VEDANTA
for
BEGINNERS

VEDANTA
for
BEGINNERS

Sri Swami Sivananda

Published by

THE DIVINE LIFE SOCIETY
P.O. SHIVANANDANAGAR—249 192
Distt. Tehri-Garhwal, Uttarakhand, Himalayas,
India

Price] 2007 [Rs. 35/-

First Edition:	1941
Second Edition:	1985
Third Edition:	1996
Fourth Edition:	2007

[1,000 Copies]

©The Divine Life Trust Society

ISBN 81-7052-046-0

ES204

Published by Swami Vimalananda for
The Divine Life Society, Shivanandanagar, and
printed by him at the Yoga-Vedanta Forest Academy
Press, P.O. Shivanandanagar, Distt. Tehri-Garhwal,
Uttarakhand, Himalayas, India

SRI SWAMI SIVANANDA

Born on the 8th September, 1887, in the illustrious family of Sage Appayya Dikshitar and several other renowned saints and savants, Sri Swami Sivananda had a natural flair for a life devoted to the study and practice of Vedanta. Added to this was an inborn eagerness to serve all and an innate feeling of unity with all mankind.

His passion for service drew him to the medical career; and soon he gravitated to where he thought that his service was most needed. Malaya claimed him. He had earlier been editing a health journal and wrote extensively on health problems. He discovered that people needed right knowledge most of all; dissemination of that knowledge he espoused as his own mission.

It was divine dispensation and the blessing of God upon mankind that the doctor of body and mind renounced his career and took to a life of renunciation to qualify for ministering to the soul of man. He settled down at Rishikesh in 1924, practised intense austerities and shone as a great Yogi, saint, sage and Jivanmukta.

In 1932 Swami Sivananda started the Sivanandashram. In 1936 was born The Divine Life Society. In 1948 the Yoga-Vedanta Forest Academy was organised. Dissemination of spiritual knowledge and training of people in Yoga and Vedanta were their aim and object. In 1950 Swamiji undertook a lightning tour of India and Ceylon. In 1953 Swamiji convened a 'World Parliament of Religions'. Swamiji is the author of over 300 volumes and has disciples all over the world, belonging to all nationalities, religions and creeds. To read Swamiji's works is to drink at the Fountain of Wisdom Supreme. On 14th July, 1963 Swamiji entered Mahasamadhi.

*Dedicated to
All Seekers of Truth*

CONTENTS

	Pages
Introduction	7
Philosophy of Raga-Dvesha	21
Adhyaropa or Superimposition	24
'I' Is the Soul and not the Body	28
Illustrations in Vedanta	30
Siva-Vidya	42
Pseudo-Vedantic Student	47
Siva-Jnanamrita Upanishad	50
Bases of Vedanta	55
Categories in Vedanta	68
Tat Tvam Asi	75
Right Significance of 'Tat Tvam Asi'	93

VEDANTA
for
BEGINNERS

INTRODUCTION

Vedanta is the culmination of the Vedas. It is entering into the study of Brahman. It is the science which raises man above the plane of worldliness. It is the rational method of meditating on the Supreme Absolute, the Eternal, the Infinite. Vedanta is the culmination of human experience and is the end of the faculty of thinking. It is the greatest and the highest knowledge. This wisdom was revealed to the ancient sages.

The Rishis and sages of yore have made experiments and researches in meditation and given to the world their spiritual experiences. These are all authoritative. You must not spend much time in making the preliminary experiments once more. Your whole life-time is not sufficient for making these experiments and researches. The experiences of sages are like ready-made compressed tablets. You will have to simply follow their instructions implicitly with perfect, unswerving faith and devotion. Then alone can you make any progress in the spiritual path and attain the goal of life.

In order to practise Sadhana for the attainment of absolute freedom, you should know in the beginning itself its technique and method. You should know the nature of bondage, the cause of bondage and the way of getting rid of bondage. You have to make a searching study of life and know its mysteries.

KARMA

You are born on this earth-plane on account of your Karmas (actions) done in previous births. This body and this condition of mind are both the results of effects of past

Karmas. What is Karma?

A Vasana or desire arises. Then you exert to possess the object. This is Karma. Thought itself is the real Karma. Physical action is only its manifestation. Then you enjoy the object. This is Bhoga. This Bhoga strengthens and fattens the Vasana. The Chakra or wheel of Vasana, Karma, Bhoga, is ever revolving. Give up Bhoga. Practise renunciation, discrimination and dispassion. Destroy the Vasanas by eradicating ignorance (Ajnana) through Brahma-Jnana, the Knowledge of the Imperishable. Then alone the wheel which binds a man to this Samsara will stop revolving. Then alone you become an Atmavan or Knower of the Self.

WHO IS A KILLER OF ATMAN?

Forgetting the Self by indulging in sensual pleasures, is killing of Atman. Even after somehow getting this rare human birth, with an innate tendency for Nivritti, he who does not strive for the liberation of his soul, is a killer of Atman. He is not an Atmavan but an Atmaha.

RENUNCIATION

The Atman can be realised only through renunciation. You have enjoyed sensual objects in millions of births. You have enjoyed sensual objects for so many years in this birth. If there has not come satisfaction in you till now, when will it come, then? Do not run after the mirage of sensual objects. The senses are deluding you. Develop dispassion and renunciation. Realise your Atman. Then only you will get eternal satisfaction, everlasting peace and immortal bliss. Wake up from your slumber of ignorance, O worldly fool!

If your body-clothes catch fire, with what celerity you want to run towards water for cooling you? You must feel like this from the burning fire of Samsara. You should feel that you are roasted in the fire of Samsara. Vairagya (dispassion) and Mumukshutva (strong yearning for liberation) should dawn in you. You should run to the Guru for saving you.

Enjoyment of objects strengthens the Vasanas or Trishnas (cravings) and makes the mind more restless. Enjoyment cannot bring satisfaction of desires. Further, Trishna drains the energy and weakens the senses.

When you dream, you see the events of fifty years within an hour. You actually feel that fifty years have passed. Which is correct, the time of one hour of waking consciousness or the fifty years of dreaming consciousness? Both are correct. The waking state and the dreaming state are of the same quality or nature. They are equal (Samana). The only difference is that the waking state is a long dream or Deerghasvapna. It will be realised that this life on earth is only a fantastic dream of the mind when the Supreme Absolute or Para-Brahman is realised.

UPASANA

Practise Upasana for acquiring concentration of mind. Upasana is of various kinds, viz., Pratika Upasana, Pratima Upasana (worship of idol), Panchakopasana (worship of the five deities: Ganesha, Siva, Vishnu, Durga and Surya), worship of Avataras like Rama and Krishna, and Ahamgraha Upasana.

Ahamgraha Upasana is Nirguna Upasana. The aspirant meditates on his own Self as Brahman. He identifies his individual self with the Supreme Self or Brahman. He tries to take out the Self that is hidden, within the body of five sheaths. Hence the significant name, 'Ahamgraha' Upasana.

'Food is Brahman'. 'Akasa is Brahman'. 'Surya (Sun) is Brahman'. 'Mind is Brahman'. 'Prana is Brahman', — All these are Upasana-Vakyas of the Upanishads. These are all Pratika Upasanas. Pratika is a symbol of Brahman. All these are symbols of Brahman. You can realise Brahman through worship of these Pratikas. You will have to feel that Brahman is hidden in these Pratikas. You will have to think that the Adhishthana or substratum of these Pratikas is Brahman. These are some of the ways of doing the Upasana of Brahman.

CONTROL OF THE SENSES

The senses should be perfectly controlled in order to be able to concentrate on Brahman. The eyes and ears also are as much turbulent and mischievous as the tongue. The eyes always want to see new forms, new scenes, new pictures and new places which the mind has heard of during conversation with other people. If you have not seen Kashmir, if you hear from those who visited Kashmir, "Kashmir is a lovely place. The springs and sceneries are wonderful," the eyes helped by the mind will agitate you again and again till you actually see Kashmir. The eyes and the ears should cease from desiring.

The two most troublesome of the senses are the tongue and the genital. One who has got an appetite for the objects of the tongue and the genital is unfit for the practice of Vedantic Sadhana. The four means of Sadhana should be well practised and only a master of these Sadhanas can take up the practice of Vedantic Sadhana.

THE MIND AND ITS WORKS

Mind is Jagat. The mind moves the senses, the Pranas, etc. Mind is the cause of bondage and liberation. A keen study of the mind and its works is necessary for the study of Vedanta.

The presiding deity of the mind is Moon or Soma. Moon is cool. It is formed of Apas-Tattva (water). Water has

INTRODUCTION

a tendency to run downwards. So also the tendency of the mind is always to run downwards towards sensual objects.

The external ear, the eye-balls, etc., are only instruments. They are not the real senses of Indriyas. The real centres or senses are in the brain or most correctly in the astral body (Sukshma Sarira). If the auditory nerve and the vision-centre in the brain are affected you can neither hear nor see. So is the case with the other senses also.

During dream the mind itself does the function of all the senses, despite the absence of the external instruments or the senses, such as eye-balls, etc. In the mind all the senses are blended. Really it is the mind that hears, tastes, feels, etc. This proves that the real senses are within. The eye-balls, tongue, external ears, nose, hands, legs, etc., are mere instruments (Karanas).

The mind does the function of Sankalpa and Vikalpa. It thinks: "Whether I can go to Dehra Dun or not?" The Buddhi or the intellect decides: "I must go." Ahamkara, the ego, arrogates. Chitta which is the store-house of Samskaras or impressions makes the preparation and gives orders to the senses. Then the senses act. The legs move. The eyes see. After you reach Dehra Dun the Vritti or wave of thought that was agitating you to see Dehra Dun subsides or gets dissolved (Laya). Then you get a temporary peace, after the gratification of your desire.

Strike a vessel made up of bell metal with the tuning fork. It will vibrate. Even so the mind vibrates if any one abuses or praises you, if you feel pain or pleasure. During praise and pleasure, the mind expands. During censure and pain it contracts.

Mind is miniature-Maya. When the functioning of the mind stops, and when the mind is dissolved into the Absolute, there is Self-realisation.

THE GURU AND THE DISCIPLE

The aspirant in olden days used to approach the Guru, with a bundle of sticks (Samit) in his hand, for spiritual instruction. What does this indicate? He prays to his preceptor, "O adorable Guru! Let my bundle of sins and worldly Vasanas be burnt in the fire of wisdom through thy grace. Let the divine flame grow in me. Let me attain the highest illumination. Make me realise, the Inner Self-effulgent Atman. Let my senses, mind, Prana and egoism be given as oblation in the fire of wisdom. Let me shine as the Light of lights!"

It is Guru's grace that removes the veil of ignorance of the disciple. The Guru's grace penetrates the heart of the disciple and raises the Brahmakara-vritti in him. The highly exalted Brahmanishtha Guru, for whom there is no world, comes down from his exalted state to teach the disciple.

VEDANTIC ETHICS

If you want to practise Vedanta or Jnana Yoga smile always, be cheerful always. He who is gloomy, he who is cheerless, he who has a castor-oil face or Sunday-face cannot become a Vedantin. He is not an Adhikari or qualified person for the practice of Vedanta. Such a man should be shut up in a cell, as he is a source of infection or contamination for others. Shun the company of such a negative person. A man of Viveka alone is fit for the practice of Vedantic Sadhana and a man of Viveka is always peaceful and joyful.

THE NATURE OF BRAHMAN

Brahman is the Absolute-Existence which is of the Nature of Knowledge-Bliss.

The world itself shines as Brahman when the veil of ignorance is torn down by the dawn of Knowledge of the Imperishable. See Brahman in your Guru, Brahman in the

INTRODUCTION

world, Brahman in everything.

In reality there is no creation. The world itself is an appearance of Brahman. The world is superimposed upon Brahman through Adhyaropa. Through Apavada-Yukti the superimposition is sublated or negated and everything is realised to be the Absolute Brahman.

Only the train moves, but you do not move. Only the boat moves, but you do not move. Even so, only the body moves, but the Indweller or the Silent Sakshi, the Witness, which is identical with the Absolute Brahman or Atman, never moves.

The word 'Atman' is used with reference to the soul in the individual. The term 'Brahman' is used with reference to the same Soul as the Soul of all beings and objects in the universe.

BRAHMAN IS BLISS

The king returns from his long journey to his palace at night. He is dead tired. He wants immediate rest. He does not want to talk even to the Maharani or the queen. The objects do not afford him any pleasure. He wants to enjoy the bliss of sleep. From where does bliss come in deep sleep, when there are no objects of enjoyment? The king (or the Jiva) in deep sleep comes in contact with the All-blissful Supreme Soul and refreshes and strengthens himself. Brahman is the source of all peace and bliss.

ISVARA AND JIVA

The causal body (Karanasarira) of the individual soul and of Isvara is one and the same. In the Jiva it is individual Avidya. Isvara's causal body is cosmic and is called Maya.

The Jiva is called Visva, Taijasa and Prajna in the three states of waking, dreaming and deep sleep experiences, and the corresponding name for the Cosmic Principle is Virat, Hiranyagarbha and Isvara. The Kutastha-Atman in the Jiva is identical with Brahman, the Absolute.

THE NATURE OF MAYA

Maya is Trigunatmika. Tamoguna is darkness and inertia. Rajoguna is passion and activity. Sattvaguna is divine light and purity.

You cannot detect your own faults on account of the force of Avidya. Avidya is the name for Maya in the individual or the Jiva. You always think that you are free from defects, that you are full of virtuous qualities, that you are the most perfect man in the world. This is Maya.

Maya is Satya or truth for a worldly-minded man. It is Anirvachaneeya or inexpressible for a Viveki or a man of discrimination. It is Tuccha or nothing for a liberated sage or Jivanmukta who is identifying himself with Satchidananda Brahman.

Vasanas and Trishnas, desires and cravings, can be destroyed in toto only by annihilating Avidya or Ajnana, the source for this Samsara, just as a tree can be destroyed only by annihilating its root. If you cut the branches of a tree, again they will grow. So you must pluck out the root itself. Avidya can be destroyed by knowledge of the Imperishable or Brahman, and not by indiscriminate suppression of the senses.

Destruction of Avidya will lead to the destruction of Raga-Dvesha. Raga and Dvesha are the modifications or effects of Avidya or ignorance.

Ajnana is absence of the Knowledge of Brahman. Just as the trees born on the soil of the mountain hide the mountain, just as the clouds born through the sun's rays hide the sun itself, so also Ajnana born from the Sakti of Brahman hides the Chaitanya or Brahman.

INTRODUCTION

Ajnana is twofold: Toola and Moola. Toola-Ajnana is ignorance in regard to the objects outside. Moola-Ajnana is ignorance covering the Self within.

THE PROJECTION OF THE WORLD

In summer the whole earth is parched. As soon as there is a shower the seeds sprout and plants come out. They were in an unmanifested state (Avyakta) before the rains. Even so the world which is in a manifested state had an unmanifested state and will become unmanifest again. It has come out of Maya, the causal body of Isvara, and will return to it in the end.

The earth, water, fire, air and ether are all productions of Maya. Water is more subtle and pervasive than earth. Fire is more subtle and pervasive than water. Air is more subtle and pervasive than fire. Akasa is more subtle and pervasive than air.

If you keep some jasmine flowers on your table, the aroma or fragrance spreads throughout the room. The fragrance is more pervasive than the flower. The flower is in one spot, but the fragrance pervades the atmosphere. The moisture of vapour is more pervasive than the earth. Sun's light is more pervasive than water. Akasa which is the mother-substance for the other four Tattvas is all-pervading. All the four elements are rooted in the all-pervading Akasa.

From Brahman or the Supreme Being sprang the five elements. Akasa was born first. Akasa is ether or space. It is Akasa or space that is the abode for the four other elements. It is the vessel or the container. There was Gati or motion in Akasa. That motion is Vayu or air. There was heat during motion of air. Fire was born from air. Fire cannot burn without air. Fire cooled and became water. Water solidified and became earth.

THE SHEATHS OF THE BODY

Five sheaths are covering the individual soul. They are the Annamaya, Pranamaya, Manomaya, Vijnanamaya and Anandamaya Kosas. The Antahkarana or the internal organ takes four forms, viz., mind, intellect, ego and subconscious mind (Chitta).

Ahamkara or the ego has connection with the intellect (Buddhi). Their abode is the Vijnanamaya Kosa. Mind (Manas) has connection with the Chitta. Their abode is the Manomaya Kosa.

The light of Surya (sun) brightens the intellect. The heat of Surya gives heat to Prana and thus maintains the heat of the body.

Just as the mind is the dividing wall between the soul and the Prana, so also Prana (vital air, energy) is the boundary-wall between the mind and the body.

Above the mind is the Buddhi. The Buddhi or intellect is made up of Agni-Tattva (fire-principle). Below the mind is Prana which is also made up of fire. Between fire (intellect above) and fire (Prana below) is the mind (water). The presiding deity of the mind is moon (Chandra). Dry up this mind (water) through the fire of Vichara (intellect), or the fire of Prana (Pranayama), or both. You will attain eternal peace, everlasting bliss.

SAMADHI

Samadhi is the Turiya or the Fourth State which is Pure Consciousness or the Supreme Absolute where even a tinge of dual consciousness does not exist.

Raja Yogis practise Nirodha-Samadhi. Jnana Yogis or Vedantins practise Badha-Samadhi. In the practice of Nirodha-Samadhi the Raja Yogi stops all the Vrittis of the mind by concentrating on one form. In the practice of Badha-Samadhi the Jnana Yogi abandons all names and

INTRODUCTION 17

forms and takes up the one essence viz., Sat-Chit-Ananda Brahman that is the substratum for all these names and forms. There is Vyapakata in the Sadhana of a Jnana Yogi. He does Sadhana even while walking. Wherever he sees he tries to see the one underlying essence and rejects the names and forms. He is in Sahaja-Samadhi even while moving. But, a Raja Yogi sits and meditates. He is in need of a steady, definite pose. He cannot be in Samadhi while walking or moving.

In Vedanta, meditation is termed as Nididhyasana. Nididhyasana leads to Sakshatkara or Nirvikalpa Samadhi. One who has experienced Nirvikalpa Samadhi will not return to the state of embodiment once again.

METHOD OF VEDANTIC SADHANA

Sravana, Manana and Nididhyasana are the three stages of Vedantic Sadhana.

Sravana is hearing of the Truth. The Abheda-Bodha-Vakya should be heard from the Brahmanishtha-Guru. Then Vedantic scriptures and treatises have to be carefully studied for the purpose of properly grasping the meaning of the great Mahavakyas.

Vedantic Granthas are of two kinds: the Pramana-granthas and the Prameya-granthas. One should always study standard works on Vedanta. A complete and exhaustive treatise on the subject has to be studied with the greatest care. Then only the full knowledge of Vedanta will dawn. Works like the Advaitasiddhi, Chitsukhi, Khandanakhandakhadya, Brahmasutras, etc., are Pramana-granthas, for they refute other theories and establish the Advaita-Tattva through logic and argumentation. Works like the Upanishads, the Bhagavadgita and the Yogavasishtha are Prameya-granthas, for they merely state the Absolute Truth with authority and do not indulge in reasoning for refuting or establishing anything. They are intuitional works, whereas the former are intellectual.

The mind should be pure and tranquil before starting Vedantic Sadhana. Keeping the Vasana in the mind is keeping a black cobra within and feeding it with milk. Your life is ever in danger. Kill these Vasanas through Vichara, Vairagya and meditation on the Atman.

The Sruti texts that deal with creation, such as "From the Atman sprang Akasa, from Akasa Vayu, from Vayu Agni," etc., are only intended for giving preliminary instructions to the neophytes or young aspirants; for they cannot grasp at once the Ajativada or the theory of non-evolution. When you read the passages which treat of creation, always remember that all this is only Adhyaropa or superimposition. Never forget this. Never think even for a second that the world is real. Only through Apavadayukti or refutation of superimposition can you establish the Kevala-Advaita-Siddhanta. If the world is real, if duality is real, you cannot have experience of Advaitic Realisation.

If the impurity of egoism or Ahamkara-Mala is destroyed, the other two impurities, viz., Kama-Mala (impurity of desire) and Karma-Mala (impurity of actions) will be destroyed by themselves. How, then, can there be Prarabdha for a Jivanmukta or the liberated sage? He is one with the Supreme Absolute.

OBSTACLES IN VEDANTIC SADHANA

Ahamkara is the greatest obstacle to Self-realisation. "I know everything. My view or opinion alone is correct. What I do is right. That man does not know anything. Everybody should follow what I say. Everybody should obey me. I am free from any kind of fault. I am full of auspicious qualities. I am very intelligent. That man is very stupid. That man is

INTRODUCTION 19

wretched. That man has got many defects. I am wise. I am beautiful." Thus says the egoistic man. This is the nature of Rajasic Ahamkara. He hides his own faults. He exaggerates and advertises his own abilities and qualities. He belittles others. He condemns others. He superimposes faults on others which they have not got. He sees not good but evil in others. He superimposes on himself several good qualities which he does not possess. That man cannot practise Vedantic Sadhana. He is unfit for the path of Jnana.

Raga and Dvesha constitute the great Samsara of the Jiva. They have to be destroyed through the knowledge of the Supreme Brahman. Either through proper understanding and discrimination or through Pratipaksha Bhavana these currents should be destroyed. Liberation is attained by simplicity, by carefulness, by purity, by controlling the passions and by following the footprints of saints and sages.

Through Vedantic Sadhana the Brahmakara-Vritti is generated. The bamboo strikes against the other bamboos and fire is generated. The whole forest is burnt. There is a huge conflagration. Then the fire subsides by itself. Even so, the Brahmakara-Vritti that is generated in the Sattvika-Manas through meditation on Brahman or the significance of the 'Tat-Tvam-Asi' Mahavakya destroys Avidya or ignorance and its effects and leads to the attainment of Brahma-Jnana, and finally dies by itself when the Supreme Brahman is realised.

The paste of *strychnos potatorum* (Nirmala seeds) removes all dirt in the water and helps it to settle at the bottom of the vessel. Along with the dirt the paste also disappears. Even so, the Brahmakara-Vritti destroys all worldly (Vishayakara) Vrittis and finally perishes by itself after the dawn of the knowledge of the Imperishable.

THE NATURE OF THE JNANI

The Jnana Yogi practises neither Pratyahara nor Chittavritti-nirodha like the Raja Yogi. He tries to behold the One Undivided Essence of Satchidananda in all names and forms. He stands as a witness or Sakshi of all the Vrittis. All Vrittis gradually die by themselves. The Jnani's method is positive (Samyagdarshana), whereas a Raja Yogi's method is negative (Nirodha).

There is no body from the Drishti or view of the sage. How can there be Prarabdha then, for a Jnani? The Jnani is one with the Absolute and hence no change takes place in his being. He is Santam, Sivam and Advaitam. He is a Jivanmukta. He is liberated in this very life itself. His body is like a burnt cloth or a sword that is changed into gold through the touch of the philosopher's stone. His ego is burnt by the fire of Supreme Wisdom.

VEDANTIC ASSERTIONS

प्रज्ञानं ब्रह्म = Consciousness is Brahman.

अहं ब्रह्मास्मि = I am Brahman.

तत्त्वमसि = That thou art.

अयमात्मा ब्रह्म = This Atman is Brahman.

सर्वं खल्विदं ब्रह्म = All this, indeed, is Brahman.

Om Santi! Santi! Santi!

PHILOSOPHY OF RAGA-DVESHA

Raga and Dvesha (likes and dislikes) only constitute this Samsara or this world of phenomena. It can be totally destroyed by knowledge of Brahman.

Raga-Dvesha is a Vasana. It has four states. Raga-Dvesha, Vasanas, Samskaras and Gunas are intertwined. They co-exist. The seat of Raga-Dvesha is the mind and the senses. Destruction of one will lead to the destruction of others. But the destruction of the source, Avidya or Ajnana, the seed of Samsara, through Brahma-Jnana will destroy everything to the very root.

The cultivation of virtues like Maitri (friendship), Karuna, (mercy), Mudita (complacency) and Upeksha (indifference) can thin out or attenuate Raga-Dvesha. This is the Pratipaksha-Bhavana method or cultivation of the opposite positive qualities, of the Raja Yogins.

Destruction of Avidya will lead to the destruction of Raga-Dvesha. Raga and Dvesha are the modifications or effects of Avidya or ignorance.

The fire of devotion also can burn in toto Raga-Dvesha.

The practice of Nishkama Karma Yoga or disinterested selfless service can thin out Raga-Dvesha to a very great extent.

Kill Raga (attachment) by the sword of Vairagya (non-attachment or dispassion or indifference to sensual objects) and Dvesha by developing cosmic love.

Raga-Dvesha assumes various forms. You like certain foods and dislike certain other foods. You like certain clothing and dislike certain other clothing. You like certain

(21)

persons and dislike certain other persons. You like certain places and dislike certain other places. You like certain sounds and dislike certain other sounds. You like certain colours and dislike certain other colours. You like soft things and dislike hard things. You like praise, respect, honour, and dislike censure, disregard, dishonour. You like a religion, view, opinion and dislike other religions, views and opinions. You like comforts, pleasures, and dislike discomforts and pain. Thus there is no peace of mind for you as the mind is ever restless and agitated. The waves of Raga-Dvesha are ever disturbing the mind. One wave of Raga-Dvesha arises in the mind and subsides after some time. Again another wave rises, and so on. There is no balance of mind. There is no peace. He who has destroyed Raga-Dvesha will be ever happy, peaceful, joyful, strong and healthy. Only he who is free from Raga-Dvesha will have a long life. Raga-Dvesha is the real cause for all diseases (Adhi and Vyadhi).

Wherever there is pleasure, there is Raga; wherever there is pain, there is Dvesha. Man wants to remain in close contact with those objects which give him pleasure. He shuns those objects which give him pain.

Though the objects that give pain are far away from you, the memory of the objects will give you pain. It is only the removal of the currents of Dvesha that will give you happiness. It is the Vritti or thought-wave that gives pain but not the objects. Hence try to destroy the current of Dvesha by developing cosmic love and Brahma-bhavana or Isvara-bhavana in all objects. Then the whole world will appear to you as the Lord in manifestation. The world or the worldly object is neither good nor bad, but it is your lower instinctive mind that makes it good or bad. Remember this point well, always. Do not find fault with the world or the objects. Find fault with your own mind.

PHILOSOPHY OF RAGA-DVESHA 23

Destruction of Raga-Dvesha means destruction of ignorance or mind and the idea of the world.

No meditation, no peace, no Samadhi is possible for a man who has not removed these two currents two foes of peace, knowledge and devotion. He who says "I enter into deep meditation. I have attained Self-realisation and Samadhi. I can also help you to enter into Samadhi" is a confirmed hypocrite. If you find in him Raga-Dvesha, attachment, hatred, prejudice, intolerance, anger, irritability, know him to be a Mithyachari. Shun his company. Remain at a respectable distance from him, because you also will catch the infection or contagion from him. Beware. Beware. Be cautious, friends!

ADHYAROPA OR SUPERIMPOSITION

Adhyaropa is superimposition! This is one of the fundamental principles of Vedanta. You cannot proceed with the study of Vedanta without understanding Adhyaropa. In reality, this world was never created. This world is superimposed on Brahman. This world is imagined where there exists only Brahman. This is Adhyaropa. This superimposition is sublated through the Yukti called Apavada.

You want to meet your friend Sri Rampratap. When you go to his house, he is not there. Somebody tells you that he has gone to a particular shop in the bazaar. You wait at his door and in a short time you see someone coming, who looks like Rampratap. From a distance you determine in your mind that the person coming is none but Rampratap. But after some time when he actually comes near you, you find that he is not Rampratap but Krishnagopal. You have superimposed Rampratap on Krishnagopal. This is Adhyaropa.

Even in case the person coming is Rampratap himself really, you think, sometimes, that the person coming is somebody else, but when he comes nearer, he happens to be Rampratap himself. This is another kind of negative superimposition. The instance in the previous case was one of positive superimposition. In each of these cases, there has been a mistaken notion that one thing is another. This is called Adhyaropa or superimposition.

Adhyaropa is the result of ignorance of the real object. Generally people mistake a rope for a snake, a post for a man, the mother-of-pearl for silver, the mirage for water,

(24)

ADHYAROPA OR SUPERIMPOSITION

etc. In hazy light of dusk you mistake a rope to be a snake. You are terribly afraid of it. But a friend of yours who comes with a light assures you that it is only a rope. Now you look at the supposed snake once again and find it to be unmoving and that it is really a rope and not snake. Now the Adhyaropa vanishes. In this instance there was no snake at all. It was only the rope that appeared as a snake. The snake was not there in the past, is not in the present and will not be there in the future (three periods of time), i.e., neither before you saw the snake, nor when you were actually seeing the snake, nor, again after your friend came with the light and assured you that it was only a rope, was there really a snake. Why was it that you saw the snake when there was only a rope? This is beyond your capacity to understand. You will simply say, it appeared to me to be a snake. So also everything that you see in this world in the form of diverse objects is only Brahman. It was Brahman only in the past and it will remain so even in the future. To a Jnani there is no world at all. This world appears to be so only to an Ajnani. Till the dawn of knowledge everyone is under the spell of ignorance only. One sees diverse objects. He feels pleasure and pain. He undergoes sufferings and tribulations. He is subject to likes and dislikes. The five organs of knowledge and the five organs of action, all work, and you cognise diverse objects, hills, mountains, rivers, men, animals, and everything else. But when, through the grace of the preceptor and through Sadhana performed untiringly until purification, through hearing, reflection and meditation, you cognise the reality, then, no more the world appears to be real. You see Brahman alone everywhere. Then you cannot hate anyone. You cannot dislike anyone, because you see your own Self or Brahman in all. Can you ever dislike yourself? You may dislike any thing second to yourself, but you cannot dislike yourself. When you see everything else also to be your Self, then whom can you hate? You will become an embodiment of pure cosmic love.

You are in search of a rope. You find one. But in the dark you mistake it to be a snake. You run away from it. You search all other places in the house and fail to find a rope. Your brother brings a light and shows you the rope which you mistook for a snake. You now see the rope. Just as you found the rope in the snake itself, even so, you will see Brahman in the objects of the world themselves. You cannot run away to the mountain-caves in search of Brahman. You have to practise seeing the Lord or Brahman in each and every object around you. When you are able to cognise the Reality underlying the objects, you will no more be deluded.

The highly exalted Brahmanishtha-Guru for whom there is no world comes down from his exalted state to teach the disciple. He is even then fully conscious of his identity with Brahman. He is fully aware that he is himself Brahman, and the disciple too. But out of compassion and love he sheds his grace on the fit disciple by imparting to him the knowledge of Brahman.

It is Adhyaropa that is to be well understood. If you can thoroughly grasp this principle, you can easily understand Vedanta. If you can dwell upon the simple truth that the whole world is merely superimposed on Brahman, if you can meditate on the idea, "This body is a house made of five elements just as a house is made of brick, cement, wood and iron; the Self within me is the Self in every other being; the flickering mind is the cause for all misery and unhappiness," you will ever rest in joy, peace and eternal bliss.

May you ever dwell upon this truth and remain happy

ADHYAROPA OR SUPERIMPOSITION

amidst all changing circumstances, joys and sorrows of the busy worldly life! May you root yourself in Brahman, the Substratum for this body, mind and soul, Jiva and Jagat, Maya and Isvara, cause and effect!

'I' IS THE SOUL AND NOT THE BODY

A sense is not soul, because you can apprehend an object through any other sense, e.g., "Previously I saw a tree and now I touch it;" — such an expression will be meaningless if 'I' is not different from the eye which cannot touch, and from the skin which cannot see. The 'I' or the Soul is distinct from the senses.

There is a fixed relation between the senses and their objects, e.g., between the eye and colour, the ear and sound, and so on. It is the eye and not the ear that can apprehend colour, and it is the ear and not the eye that can apprehend sound. If a sense were the Soul, it (the Soul) could apprehend only one object, but the 'I' can apprehend many objects; the 'I' can see colour, hear sound, and so on. Therefore, the 'I' or the Soul which confers unity on the various kinds of apprehension is different from the senses, each of which can apprehend only one object.

If we do not admit a permanent Soul beyond our frail body, we shall be confronted with many absurdities such as loss of merited action *(Kritahani)* and gain of unmerited action *(Akritabhyagama)*. A man who has committed a certain sin may not suffer its results in this life, and unless there is a Soul continuing in the next life, he will not suffer them at all. This is loss of merited action. Again, we often find a man suffering the results of actions which he never did in this life. This would be a gain of unmerited action, unless we believe that his Soul did exist previous to this life and that he did the action in his previous life.

A thing seen previously by the left eye is recognised

now by the right eye. This would have been impossible if the Soul were identical with the left eye alone or the right eye alone, on the principle that the seat of recognition must be the same as the seat of perception. Hence we must admit that there is a Soul which is distinct from the left and right eyes and which is the common seat of perception and recognition.

The Soul is distinct from the senses, because there is an excitement of one sense through the operation of another sense. When you see a mango fruit or lime pickle, there is salivation in our mouth. The sense of taste is excited. There is an excitement of the sense of taste on account of the operation of the sense of sight. This would be impossible unless there is a Soul distinct from the senses and uniting the senses. The Soul sees the fruit or the pickle and remembers its properties. The remembrance of the properties of the object excites the sense of taste.

You can remember only that object which you have seen. You remember the smell of an object by seeing its colour. This would be impossible if remembrance is a quality of a sense, e.g., the eye, which has never smelt the object. Therefore, remembrance must be admitted to be a quality of a distinct entity called the Soul which is the common seat of perception of colour and smell. The Soul is the absolute Seer and is Consciousness in nature, whereas all other things, — objects, body, senses, Pranas, mind, intellect, etc., are the seen and are inert in nature. The Soul is the Imperishable Reality, while everything else is perishable and false.

ILLUSTRATIONS IN VEDANTA

(Nyayas)

The Vedanta Philosophy is best taught through practical illustrations of daily life, because its abstract truths cannot be understood by the finite intellect very easily. The main purport of Vedanta is that Brahman alone is real and the whole world of appearance is unreal, and that the Jiva is nothing but Brahman Itself. This abstruse theory cannot be comprehended by ordinary men of small understanding, who are immersed in the life of relativity and ignorance. They are taught this sublime Truth by means of illustrations suitable to them, so that they may fix their minds on the Reality through various angles of vision.

Section I

1. RAJJUSARPA-NYAYA

In the twilight a man treads upon a rope, and mistaking it for a poisonous snake, jumps in hurry, and cries out in fear. His heart throbs quickly. But when a light is brought by a friend of his, he finds that it is not a snake but only a rope, and then all his fears vanish. This is to illustrate the unreality of the world and its superimposition on the supreme Brahman. Brahman is the Reality and the world is only a superimposition on Brahman just as the snake is a superimposition on the rope.

2. MRIGATRISHNA-NYAYA

In the desert a traveller sees at noon a mirage where water, meadows, trees and mansions are seen. He believes the sight to be a true one and pursues the spot. The nearer he thinks he is to the spot the further it retreats from him.

He leaves his way out far and wanders in the desert. Then he realises that he has done a mistake in straying away from his path in search of this false appearance of water. He once again does not get deceived by this kind of mirage. This is given, in Vedanta, to illustrate the falsity of the universe which appears to give pleasure, with objects for indulgence, to the wanderer, the Jiva. When the Jiva realises through Jnana or Knowledge of the Self, that this world is unreal and that he had done a mistake in turning away from the true path leading to his original State of Perfection or Svarupa, he stops from running after the false mirage of this life of sensual pleasure on earth. The world is only an appearance, just like a mirage which is only an appearance of sun's rays.

3. SHUKTIRAJATA-NYAYA

This is similar to 'Akashanilima-Nyaya' or 'Stambha-Nara-Nyaya' (Man in the post). These are also similar to Rajjusarpa-Nyaya. These illustrate the superimposition of the unreal on the real. The mother-of-pearl is mistaken for pure silver, the attributeless sky appears blue, the post is mistaken for a man at night. The knowledge of the Supreme Brahman, the Reality, comes after proper understanding, through discrimination, patience, endurance, renunciation and meditation. The world is an appearance of Brahman, just as the man in the post is only an appearance of the post, and the silver in nacre an appearance of nacre.

4. KANAKAKUNDALA-NYAYA

This is similar to Mrittika-Ghata-Nyaya and the analogy of iron and implements. All the ornaments are made of one type of gold, but they are of diverse forms. They are all gold only in reality. There are various kinds of jars, pots and vessels, big and small, round and narrow, and of all forms, but all of them are but mud in reality. Various kinds of implements and tools are manufactured, with various forms and uses, but all of them are iron only in reality. The names of those various formations and their forms are false, since they are, in reality, only the original source, the gold, mud or iron. This is to illustrate that the various names and forms of this world and its contents are simply false, for all are in essence Brahman only. Brahman alone is appearing in many names and forms.

5. SAMUDRATARANGA-NYAYA

There are countless waves rolling in the vast ocean. Each wave is distinguished from the other and each wave can be perceived separately, one by one. But all are water only, and are not separate from the great ocean. All are one only in reality. The difference is only apparent. This illustrates that all the innumerable Jivas that appear in this universe, though apparently they are perceived to be separate from one another, are in reality that one Ocean of Satchidananda and are all identical with it. There is no difference or diversity.

6. SPHATIKAVARNA-NYAYA

This is the analogy of colour in crystals. The Sphatika or the brilliant crystal is pure in itself and has no particular colour of its own. But when a coloured object is brought near it, it reflects the same colour and itself appears to be of that colour,—blue, red or whatever it be. In the same manner, Brahman or the Atman is colourless, taintless and attributeless, but only the Upadhis or the limiting adjuncts make it appear as different and of various qualities, names and forms.

7. PADMAPATRA-NYAYA

This is the analogy of the lotus-leaf and water. Rain water often falls on a lotus-leaf but the water drips down

ILLUSTRATIONS IN VEDANTA 33

and the leaf does not get stained by or attached to the water on it. In the same manner, this Atman or Brahman is untainted, though there are countless worlds rolling in it, and countless bodies are seen to be put on by it.

8. VATAGANDHA-NYAYA

The wind carries whatever scent is exposed to it and spreads it everywhere. But the air is pure and is not defiled by bad scent or ornamented by a good scent therein. This is similar to the illustration of the lotus-leaf and water to show the unattached state of the Atman or the Brahman, though it puts on various names, forms and actions in the appearance of phenomena.

9. OORNANABHI-NYAYA

The spider brings forth the thread from its mouth to weave its web and withdraws it again into its mouth. But the thread is nothing but the body of itself and is one with it. Even so this world is projected forth by Brahman and then again withdrawn by Brahman. But the world is nothing but the Being of Brahman only appearing. This shows that all is Brahman alone in reality.

10. SURYA-BIMBA-NYAYA

There is only one sun illumining all the worlds. But there are perceived as many different reflections of the sun, as there are ponds, tanks, rivers, mirrors, etc. The sun is reflected in all waters, but there is only one real Sun. So also there is only one Supreme Existence-Absolute, the infinite Brahman, but that One Reality is reflected through the Upadhis of Maya and Avidya as various worlds and Jivas. This is false, for it is only the appearance of reflections. The Truth is only One.

11. GHATAKASA-NYAYA

This is the analogy of ether in a pot. There is the great

Ether or the Mahakasa pervading the whole universe and there is the same ether inside a jar also. But the ether in a jar can be differentiated from the great ether on account of the ether being enclosed and contained by the jar. But the ether is in no way affected even in the least by the partitions made by the walls of the jar. When the jar is broken the ether in the jar becomes one with the great ether, having undergone no change at any time. Even so, the Atman in the individual is partitioned by the mind and the body, but, in reality, it is one with the great Paramatman, the Supreme Soul. When the body is broken and the mind is destroyed the Atman becomes one with the Supreme Brahman, having undergone no change due to the appearance of the mind and the body, the products of Avidya or Upadhi or ignorance.

12. BHRAMARA-KITA-NYAYA

The Bhramara or the wasp is said to sting the insects or the Kitas which it brings to its hive and through stinging them and poisoning them makes them feel its presence alone everywhere, at all times. The insects, so to say, meditate on the presence of the wasp, at all times, and in turn become wasps themselves thereby. This is to show that by meditating on the formula *'Aham Brahma Asmi'* or 'I am Brahman' the Jiva becomes Brahman itself in the end.

13. DAGDHAPATA-NYAYA

This is the analogy of the burnt cloth. If a cloth is burnt you will see, even afterwards, that there is the same form of the cloth appearing. But when touched with the hand even slightly, it is reduced to ashes. Even so is the body of the Jnani or the Jivanmukta. He does possess a body, but it is like the burnt cloth. It only appears, but it has no reality. It is burnt by the fire of Wisdom and there is no ego to sustain it. The Jnani is untouched by worldly taints and

ILLUSTRATIONS IN VEDANTA

leaving that appearance of a body he attains Sadyo-Mukti or Kaivalya-Mukti.

14. ARUNDHATI-NYAYA

To show to a person the star Arundhati in the sky, one points out at first to a big star above and says that that big star is Arundhati. The person is first led to a big star that is clearly seen and is said that that is the Arundhati. Then after rejecting that star the real star is shown. Even so, the aspirant is at first shown a physical method of approaching the Reality through service and formal worship of forms, but afterwards he is led gradually to the Supreme Truth which is formless and impersonal.

15. BIJA-VRIKSHA-NYAYA

The seed is the cause of the tree and the tree is the cause of the seed. It cannot be said which is the cause of which. This is to illustrate that every question and statement has got a counter-question and counter-statement, that every *this* is also every *that*, that the whole world is bound in relativity, and that the Ultimate Truth is Silence, which Dakshinamurti followed.

16. MARKATA-KISHORA-NYAYA

The child of a monkey catches hold of the mother's breast and never leaves it even in times of extreme danger. It does not rely upon the mother for its safety, but struggles for itself. This is to illustrate the nature of the aspirant on the path of Jnana-Sadhana, who does not rely upon any external help or grace for his salvation, but struggles for himself and attains Wisdom of the Self.

17. ASHMA-LOSHTA-NYAYA

This is the analogy of stone and mud. Mud is very hard when compared to cotton but it is very soft when compared to stone. This is to show that a thing may be bad as compared with better things, but is good when compared with inferior things, and vice versa. This is used to illustrate that there is no quality in things by themselves, that there is no plurality in life, and that difference is caused only through imagination.

18. KAKADANTA-NYAYA

This is akin to Vandhya-putra-Nyaya, Gaganaaravinda-Nyaya, Gandharvanagara-Nyaya or Shashavishna-Nyaya. It is useless to search for the teeth of a crow, for it has no teeth. Similar is the case with the son of a barren woman, a lotus grown in the sky, a city in the clouds, and the horns of a hare. This is to show that it is meaningless to question about the contradictions and mysteries of existence like "Why did the Perfect God create an imperfect world?" etc., for there is no real change and there is no creation at all in reality, and that these questions arise so long as the Sun of Wisdom has not arisen.

19. DANDAPOOPA-NYAYA

When many cakes are tied to a stick and one says, "the stick has been pulled down and is not to be found", it naturally follows that the cakes also are missing. This is to illustrate that all doubts are cleared and desires pacified when it is known that Existence is Eternal, Infinite and Changeless, Undivided, Intelligence and Bliss! For, doubts and desires arise only when there is change or evolution.

20. KSHAURIKAPUTRA-NYAYA

A king asked a barber to bring the most beautiful boy in his kingdom. The barber searched in the whole country but could not find a really beautiful one. He felt very sorry and came to his house in distress. But finding his own son in his house, who was actually an embodiment of ugliness, he thought that his son was the most beautiful in the world and brought him to the king. This is to illustrate that whatever is dear to one and whatever is one much attached to, is found to be the best and the most precious and that men have love only for the world, as they are strongly attached to it. Everyone is shut up within his own limited individual experience.

21. VISHA-KRIMI-NYAYA

Worms revelling in poisonous substances are not affected by that poison and are happy there. This is to denote that, though a thing is worthless and low to one, it may be very good to another and may be the very thing that the other wants and craves for, and also vice versa. It illustrates that creatures of the world are happy in it, for they know not anything higher.

22. KAKATALIYA-NYAYA

A crow came and sat on a palmyra tree, and just at that time, a fruit of that tree fell on its head and killed it. The falling of the fruit had really no connection with the crow's sitting on the tree. The coincidence of the two events was merely accidental. This illustration is used to describe anything which is purely accidental and has no reason behind. It is said in the Yogavasishtha that the appearance of a common world to many Jivas, each of whom has really an independent world of itself, is only accidental (Kakataliya) and has no reason or any other meaning for it whatsoever.

Section II

1. BUTTER IN MILK

Butter or ghee exists in milk. But where is it? It cannot be perceived. But it is present everywhere in milk, in each and every drop of milk. There is no particle of milk where butter or ghee is not present. In the same manner Brahman is present everywhere; and there is no speck of space where Brahman is not. But Brahman cannot be perceived and It seems to be nowhere. It is the very essence of cream of existence, but It is nowhere to the eyes of a worldly-minded man. This illustrates the omnipresence of Brahman.

2. FIRE IN WOOD

Fire is present in all parts of wood, just like butter in milk. It is only one fire that is existent in all woods, but it becomes various in name, form and action when it manifests into visible fire. Even so Brahman which is the Reality in all things appears as many in name, form and action when manifest in various Jivas and countless worlds. But the Truth is only One; it only appears to be many.

3. SMOKE AND FIRE

Smoke emanates from fire. The dense smoke covers the bright fire and the fire cannot be seen. But the smoke comes only from the fire and is only a part of the burning fire. It is one with fire. Similarly Maya projects itself forth in the being of Brahman and clouds the appearance of Brahman so that Brahman is not perceived and there is variety in existence. But Maya is one with Brahman and is Brahman only appearing, the Effulgent, Consciousness-Bliss.

4. THREAD AND NECKLACE

The necklace contains many beads of various forms, but there is one single thread that connects them all and keeps them in unity. The thread is their very support and being. Even so in the diverse Jivas and worlds that exist, there is one common Life-Principle, the Supreme Brahman, as it is called, that unifies the entirety of Existence, and is the very support and being of all that is.

ILLUSTRATIONS IN VEDANTA

5. WEARER AND APPAREL

The old and used clothes are thrown away and new clothes are put on by man. In the Bhagavadgita this is given to illustrate that the Jiva throws off an old and used-up body and assumes a new one, and that the Jiva therefore does never die in reality.

6. THE CHAMELEON

The chameleon is an animal which changes its colour at any time according to the colour of the surface it moves on. A person who has seen the chameleon when it is assuming the colour red says that the chameleon is red. But the other one who has seen it only when it is assuming the colour green says that the chameleon is green. But a person who has watched the chameleon all along, carefully, under the tree, knows all its colours, and does not have any more doubts. This is to illustrate that people who have only a partial understanding of the Nature of God quarrel among themselves that this is right and this is wrong, God is like this, God is like that, etc. But a Brahma-Jnani who has calmly watched the nature of the whole existence knows its true nature and does not have any more doubts regarding the nature of the Absolute.

7. SALT AND WATER

A particle of salt dropped in a large vessel of water dissolves itself in the water and is no more perceivable to the eye. But any part of that water, if tasted, is felt to be saltish. In the same manner the Jiva, on attaining Wisdom, dissolves itself in the ocean of Existence-Knowledge-Bliss and becomes one with the All. All is felt to be the Supreme Bliss. It is everywhere the same.

8. TWO THORNS

If a thorn gets stuck to the leg, it is carefully removed

with the help of another thorn. But after the work is over, both the thorns are thrown away and one becomes happy. Even so, the evil qualities and ignorance born of Avidya should be removed by virtuous qualities and knowledge and after attaining Peace, one has to discard them both and transcend all differences.

9. SWORD AND PHILOSOPHER'S STONE

At the very touch of a philosopher's stone the sharp iron sword is turned into gold and afterwards it does not cut, even if it has the appearance of a sword. Even so, the ego of the Siddha-Jnani or the Jivanmukta, though it has the appearance of individuality and presents a physical body, cannot bind the Siddha again to rebirth, for it is transformed into Suddha-Sattva by the touch of the Supreme Wisdom of the Absolute.

10. CHANDELIER AND ELECTRICITY

In a chandelier various bulbs of different colour are seen and there is a grand diversity in their forms. But the basis of the entire light is the one power of electricity charged from the dynamo, which is the common force of all bulbs, and which has no colours of varieties. Even so, there are various worlds and creatures of multifarious names and forms, but all are having their basis or support in the one Power, the Supreme Brahman which is Indivisible and Attributeless, Nameless and Formless.

11. THE TWO BIRDS

Two birds live in the same tree as comrades. But one of them eats the sweet fruit of the tree and gets bound in delusion. But the other bird does not eat anything and remains an eternal witness. This analogy occurs in the Rigveda and the Mundaka Upanishad. This is to illustrate that the Jiva and the Paramatman are both in the same body, but the Jiva enjoys through contact the pleasures

ILLUSTRATIONS IN VEDANTA

and pains of Samsara and gets bound, whereas the Paramatman or the Supreme Soul, the Kutastha, remains as a Sakshi or a witness and exists ever in Absoluteness.

12. MAN AND THE NECKLACE

A person wears round his neck a gold necklace and in excitement and confusion searches for that necklace here and there. He walks and runs this side and that side but nowhere does he find the necklace, though it is around his own neck. Similarly, the individual or the Jiva searches for Perfection and Bliss outside, everywhere, forgetting the fact that the Immortal Seat or Brahman is its very being itself and that it is identical with that Brahman.

13. SILK-WORM AND THE COCOON

The silk-worm projects forth a certain thread from its mouth and then binds itself within a cocoon. Similarly, the Jiva binds itself through ignorance and attachment, and suffers from the bondage of embodied life through births and deaths.

Om Shanti! Shanti! Shanti!

SIVA-VIDYA

Khanda I

NATURE OF BRAHMAN

Om! Brahman or Siva or the Impersonal Absolute is the Source and Substratum for the world of phenomena. He is the Source of the Vedas. From Him this world proceeds. In Him it lives. In Him it gets dissolved. He is Eternal, Self-existent, Self-luminous and Self-contained. He is all-Full. He is beyond Time, Space and Causation. He is birthless, deathless and decayless.

Khanda II

CONTRADICTIONS RECONCILED

He moves and moves not. He moves in His manifested or Saguna aspect. He moves not in His transcendental aspect. He is smaller than the smallest and greater than the greatest. He is smaller than the smallest because He is the Soul of even the ant, the mustard and the atom, and He is extremely subtle. He is greater than the greatest because He is the Soul of this entire universe and extends beyond this universe, also and He is Infinite. He is nearer than the nearest and farther than the farthest. He is nearer to the thirsty aspirants, but He is farther to those who are worldly-minded. He is nearer than the nearest because He is the Inner Soul of everything. He is farther than the farthest because He is Infinite. He is beyond the reach of the mind and the senses (Avangmanogochara). He cannot be reached by people of gross mind and outgoing senses. But He can be attained by that aspirant who is endowed with a subtle, sharp, one-pointed intellect

(Manasaivaanudrashtavyam), and who is equipped with four means, and the grace and the instructions of a Brahma-Srotri, Brahma-Nishtha Guru, in Tat-Tvam-Asi Mahavakya.

Khanda III

VISION OF A SAGE AND OF A WORLDLY MAN

Brahman is the only Reality. He is the only living Truth. The Liberated Sage or Jivanmukta beholds Brahman only everywhere. There is no world for him in the three periods of time. But the ignorant man sees only the five elements and the forms. The world of names and forms only is real for him. He denies Brahman altogether.

Khanda IV

SUPERIMPOSITION (ADHYASA)

The man who moves in a desert in the noon sees the mirage at some distance and mistakes it for water. He runs there to drink water but is disappointed. The rays of the sun fall on the bed of sand and generate the mirage. The mirage appears as a sheet of water and deludes man. Even so the worldly man beholds the five elements and their combination, i.e., names and forms, on account of Avidya. Avidya hides the real and makes the unreal appear as real.

In the twilight a man mistakes a rope for a snake, gets frightened and cries. When a friend brings a light his fear vanishes. He sees a rope only. Even so a worldly man mistakes the impure, perishable body for the Pure, Imperishable Atman and suffers in diverse ways on account of this erroneous notion or superimposition (Adhyasa) caused by Avidya. When the Avidya is destroyed through Brahma-Jnana or Knowledge of the Eternal through initiation into the significance of "Tat-Tvam-Asi" Mahavakya by the Preceptor or Brahma-Vidya Guru, he becomes identical with the Supreme Soul. The world of names and forms vanishes in toto. He sees Brahman only. All his fears terminate.

Khanda V

HAPPINESS IS IN THE ATMAN ONLY

The feeling of pleasure is an internal feeling. There is no pleasure in physical objects, though they excite pleasure in man. Sensual pleasure is only a reflection of the Bliss of the Atman. When a desire is gratified the mind moves towards the Atman and rests in the Atman for a very short time, and the man experiences pleasure. Atman or Brahman only is the embodiment of Bliss (Ananda Svarupa). Atman is full of Bliss (Anandamaya). Atman is a Mass of Bliss (Ananda-Ghana).

Khanda VI

BRAHMAN IS BOTH MATERIAL AND EFFICIENT CAUSE

Brahman is both the material and the efficient cause of this universe (Abhinna-Nimitta-Upadana-Karana). He is the fictitious material cause (Vivarta-Upadana). He somehow appears as this universe through Maya, without Himself being affected in the least, by names and forms. This is a mystery. This is indescribable.

Khanda VII

BRAHMAN IS UNATTACHED

Just as the crystal is not affected by the coloured objects, though it reflects them, just as the sun is not affected by the defects of the eye and other objects, just as ether is not affected, by reason of its subtlety, so, seated everywhere in the body, this Atman is not affected.

SIVA-VIDYA

Khanda VIII

QUALIFICATIONS OF AN ASPIRANT

He who is equipped with the four means, who has purified his heart through selfless service (Nishkama Karma Yoga); service of Guru, Japa, Kirtan and Upasana, who is calm, dispassionate, reflective, discriminative, fearless, straightforward, humble, large-hearted, compassionate, generous, truthful, pure and who is free from pride, egoism, arrogance, will realise this Mysterious, Indescribable, Unthinkable Brahman or the Imperishable.

Khanda IX

KAIVALYA

Kaivalya-Mukti or final emancipation can be attained through knowledge of Brahman. Krama-Mukti is attained through Bhakti.

Mukti is not a thing to be achieved or attained. It is already there. You will have to know that you are free, by removing the veil of ignorance.

Khanda X

METHOD OF MEDITATION

I am All-blissful Siva	OM!
I am Immortal Brahman	OM!
I am Existence-Knowledge-Bliss Absolute (Satchidananda Svarupoham)	OM!
I am Infinite (Ananta)	OM!
I am Eternal (Nitya)	OM!
I am ever pure (Suddha)	OM!
I am perfect (Siddha)	OM!
I am ever free (Mukta)	OM!
I am unattached (Asanga)	OM!
I am witness (Sakshi)	OM!

I am non-doer (Akarta)   OM!
I am non-enjoyer (Abhokta)   OM!
I am not this body   OM!
I am not this Prana   OM!
Satchidananda-Svarupoham   OM!

This is the Quintessence of Kevala-Advaita Vedanta or Absolute Monism.

Thus ends the glorious Siva Vidya! OM!

PSEUDO-VEDANTIC STUDENT

A young aspirant says: "I have taste for Vedanta only. I do not like either Bhakti or Karma Yoga. They are far inferior to Vedanta. Only Vedanta elevates me. Only Vedanta inspires me and raises me to the magnanimous heights of Divine Splendour and Glory."

This foolish Vedantic student is like the greedy typhoid patient with ulcers in his bowels, who wants to eat and says, "I have taste for sweetmeats. I want to eat them now." What will be the result if he eats Rasagullas and Laddus at this stage? The bowels will rupture and he will die of bleeding from the bowels or intestinal haemorrhage immediately.

He is also like the patient who selects himself a medicine from the almirah, Liquor Arsenicalis or Tr. of Opium, and says, "I like this medicine only. I want to taste this now." What will happen if he tastes this medicine without consulting the doctor? He will die of arsenical or opium poisoning. He does not know the dose of the medicine. Instead of taking a few drops he may take them in a large quantity and give up his vital breath at once. It is the doctor alone who can select the right medicine for the patient.

Everybody cannot want to become a Commissioner or District Collector or Governor without possessing the necessary qualifications. Can anyone become an M.A., Ph.D., without undergoing the course for Matriculation, F.A. and B.A.?

It is the Guru alone who can select the right type of Yoga for the aspirant and right kind of books for him. He knows the degree of evolution of the student and he alone can chalk out the right path for the aspirant. He will ask him to study first Atma-Bodha, Tattva-Bodha, Atma-Anatma-Viveka. But the raw self-willed student goes to the library and at once takes up the highly advanced books, Yoga-Vasishtha and Brahma-Sutras, for his study! He becomes a pseudo-Vedantin or lip-Vedantin within six months and enters into discussions with elderly aspirants.

A little knowledge is a dangerous thing. After studying Yoga-Vasishtha and the Karikas on Mandukya Upanishad for six months, he says: "There is no world in the three periods of time. Aham Brahma Asmi—Sivoham—Sivah Kevaloham." He is puffed up with empty pride, vanity and hollowness, and walks in the streets with his head erect. He will never make any prostration to elderly Sannyasis and Sadhus, but chant the formula very often, "Sivoham, Sivoham."

Such aspirants are formidable Asuras on this earth. They are a great burden on this earth. They pollute the atmosphere and create dissensions and quarrels everywhere, by entering into heated debates with sincere devotees and Karma Yogis. They cannot prosper in the spiritual path.

Vedanta in the hands of raw and unregenerate persons who lack purity and devotion and who have not removed the impurity of their hearts through untiring selfless service with Atma-Bhava and Kirtan and prayer, is perilous. It is like a sharp razor in the hands of a child. Instead of expanding their hearts the Vedantic study will thicken and fatten their egoism. They fall into the deep abyss of ignorance. There is no hope, for them, of being lifted up, as their heart is filled with foolish, Tamasic, obstinacy, false Vedantic pride and self-superiority and false Tushti (satisfaction).

May this land be free from such impotent, pseudo lip-Vedantins! May this world abound with real Vedantins like Dattatreya, Yajnavalkya and Sankara!

SIVA-JNANAMRITA UPANISHAD

ॐ भद्रं कर्णेभिः शृणुयाम देवाः
भद्रं पश्येमाक्षभिर्यजत्राः ।
स्थिरैरंगैस्तुष्टुवांसस्तनूभिः
व्यशेम देवहितं यदायुः ॥
ॐ शान्तिः शान्तिः शान्तिः

Om! O gods! may we, with our ears, hear what is auspicious! O ye, fit to be worshipped! May we, with our eyes, see what is auspicious! May we enjoy the life allotted to us by the gods, offering our praise with our bodies strong of limbs!

Om Peace Peace Peace!

MANTRA 1

यदेतन्नामरूपात्मकं जगत् तदाभासमात्रम् । न तद् ब्रह्मणः पुरस्तात् प्रतितिष्ठति । रज्जुसर्पन्यायेन ब्रह्मणि जगतोऽध्यासःदेहाध्यायसश्च ॥१॥

1. This world of names and forms is a mere appearance. It has no independent existence apart from Brahman. Just as a snake is superimposed on the rope, this world and body are superimposed on Brahman.

यथा रज्जुज्ञानात् सर्पभ्रान्तिर्निवर्तते सह तन्मूलेन भयेन तथा ब्रह्मज्ञानान्निवर्ततेऽविद्या सहैव जनिमरणभयेन ॥२॥

2. Just as knowledge of a rope removes the illusion of a snake in the rope and the consequent fear, so also the knowledge of the Self (Brahman) removes Avidya or ignorance and the fear of birth and death.

(50)

तद् ब्रह्म तत् सच्चिदानन्दस्वरूपं स्वयंज्योतिर्नित्यं अनाद्यन्तं निर्विकारं अमृतं अभयं निरंजनम् ॥३॥

3. Brahman is Sat-Chit-Ananda Svarupa. It is self-luminous (Svayam-Jyoti). It is eternal (Nityam), beginningless (Anadi), endless (Ananta), changeless (Nirvikara), deathless (Amritam), fearless (Abhayam) and spotless (Niranjana).

निर्गुणं निराकारं निर्विशेषं अखण्डं निरुपाधिकं एकमेवाद्वितीयं स्वतन्त्रं नित्यमुक्तं परिपूर्णम् ॥४॥

4. Brahman is attributeless (Nirguna), formless, (Nirakara), without special characteristics (Nirvisesha), without parts (Akhanda), without any limiting adjunct (Nirupadhika), one without a second (Ekam eva Advitiyam), independent (Svatantra), ever free (Nitya-mukta) and all-full (Paripurna).

शरीरत्रयव्यतिरिक्तं, पञ्चकोशेभ्यः पृथक्, अवस्थात्रयसाक्षिभूतं, त्रिगुणातीतं, द्वन्द्वनिर्मुक्तम्। सच्चिदानन्दात्मकं, सर्वत्रसारभूतं, अन्तःकरणस्य योनिः तथा प्राणेन्द्रियशरीराणां अस्य च जगतः ॥५॥

5. Brahman is distinct from the three bodies and five sheaths (Koshas). He is the silent witness of the three states. He transcends the three Gunas and the pairs of opposites. He is an embodiment of Sat-Chit-Ananda. He is the essence or Swarupa. He is the source or womb for the mind, Prana, Indriyas, body and this world.

ओमित्येष प्रणवो ब्रह्मणः प्रतीकः। वीर्यवच्चैतस्योच्चारणं ओंकारादेष प्रपञ्चः संवृत्तः। ओंकारे प्रतितिष्ठति। ओंकारे च प्रलीयते महाप्रलये। ओंकारे प्रतितिष्ठति। ओंकारे च प्रलीयते महाप्रलये। ओंकारश्चतुर्णां वेदानां सारभूतः ॥६॥

6. Om or the Pranava is the symbol (Pratika) of Brahman. It is the word of power. From Om this world is

projected; in Om it exists and in Om it is involved during cosmic Pralaya. Om is the essence of the four Vedas.

योऽसौ प्रयत्नमानः साधनचतुष्टयसंपन्नः निरस्तचित्तदोषः स्थिरीकृतचित्तवृत्तिः सात्त्विकगुणविशिष्टः स एव ज्ञानयोगमर्हति ॥७॥

7. That aspirant who is endowed with the four means, who has removed impurities and tossing of the mind, who is equipped with Sattvic virtues is only fit for the path of Jnana Yoga.

जाग्रतया प्रयत्नसाधितेन दीर्घेणाविच्छिन्नेन ध्यानेन यथाक्रमं भूमिकाः समारोहेत्। अप्राप्य च भूमानं नाभियोगादि्विरमेत्। सविकल्पसमाधिमात्रेण सन्तोषाभासमुपलभ्य न साधनमपहस्तयेत् ॥८॥

8. By careful, diligent, protracted and unceasing practice of meditation gradually ascend the steps (Bhumikas). Do not relax the efforts till you attain the Bhuma (Highest). Do not stop the Sadhana when you get some false contentment from the Savikalpa Samadhi.

सानुभवं सार्थानुसंधानं च प्रणवमाम्रेडयन्। अध्यात्ममार्गे तरति सर्वान्तरायान्। ह्रस्वः प्रणवः सर्वपापनोदनः। दीर्घो मुक्तिप्रदः। प्लुतोऽखिलसिद्धिहेतु ॥९॥

9. Repetition of Om with meaning and Bhava will remove all obstacles in the spiritual path. The Hrasva (short) Pranava destroys all sins. The Dirgha (long) Pranava gives Mukti, the Pluta gives all Siddhis.

'तत्त्वमसि'-महावाक्यस्य लक्ष्यार्थानुसन्धानमात्मबोधस्यातित्वरितः पन्थाः ॥१०॥

10. Meditation on Lakshyartha (indicative meaning) of Tat Tvam Asi (That Thou Art) Mahavakya (great sentence) is the direct means for attaining Self-realisation.

साधनचतुष्टयसंपन्नो मुमुक्षुः श्रोत्रियाद् ब्रह्मनिष्ठात् अधीत्य श्रुतिः

SIVA-JNANAMRITA UPANISHAD

षड्लिंगप्रतिपत्त्या ब्रह्मविचारं कृत्वा ध्यानसमाधी अनुप्रविशेत् ॥११॥

11. That aspirant who is endowed with the four means, should hear the Srutis from a Brahma-srotri—Brahmanishtha and enquire into the nature of Brahman through the help of Shad Lingas and then reflect and meditate.

साधनचतुष्टयसंपन्नस्य साधकस्य मुमक्षोः सात्त्विकभावप्रभवा ब्रह्माकारवृत्तिः अज्ञानावरणं विभिद्य स्वयमपि नश्यति ॥१२॥

12. The Brahmakara Vritti that arises from the Sattvic mind of the aspirant who is equipped with the four means destroys the veil of ignorance and dies by itself.

मनश्चापि जडम्। सत्त्वगुणकार्यभूतम्। ब्रह्मणो मूलभूतात् स्वप्रकाशमादत्ते। तदेतत् सादि च सान्तं च। ॥१३॥

13. Mind also is Jada. It is an effect (Karya) of Sattva Guna. It borrows its light from its source, Brahman. It has a beginning and an end.

तिस्रो भावनाः, निद्रा, चित्तविक्षेपो, विषयासक्तिः, चित्तावसादो, मनोराज्यं, व्याधिरित्यादयो नित्यमात्मसाक्षात्कारस्यान्तरायाः ॥१४॥

14. The three Bhavanas, sleep, tossing of mind, mind running towards objects, depression, building castles in the air, diseases, etc., are the chief obstacles in the attainment of Self-realisation.

साक्षात्कृतपरिपूर्णस्वरूपो ज्ञानी सर्वप्राणिजातमात्मनि, सर्वस्मिन्नपि प्राणिजाते चात्मानं पश्यति। तस्मै ब्रह्मणोऽन्यत् किमपि न विद्यते। स निःशंकं लोके संचरति ॥१५॥

15. The Jnani who has full Self-realisation sees all beings in the Self and the Self in all beings. There is nothing other than Brahman for him. He moves about fearlessly in the world.

स्वसंकल्पमहिम्ना ज्ञानी सर्वमिच्छाविधेयमधिगच्छति । यदनुसंदध्यात् तस्य तदेवाविर्भवति । स महामहिम्नामाकरः ॥१६॥

16. A Jnani gets anything he likes through the power of his Sat-Sankalpa (perfect will). A Jnani wills and everything comes into being. A Jnani has tremendous powers.

ज्ञानाधिगमे कर्मणां प्रविलयः । ज्ञानिनः प्रारब्धकर्मापि न विद्यते ॥१७॥

17. When one gets Jnana, all Karmas are destroyed. There is no Prarabdha (fructifying) Karma for a Jnani.

जीवत एव ज्ञानिनः तुरीयातीतदशायां विदेहमुक्तिर्भवति ॥१८॥

18. Videha Mukti comes when a Jnani is living. A Jnani gets disembodied salvation (Videha Mukti) when he enters the state of Turiyatita, the Absolute.

त्रैकालिकं ज्ञानं सर्वतो निर्भयता, सर्वथा निष्कामता, कथंचिदपि पीडानधिगमः, समतादृष्टिः द्वन्द्वेषु समता, अत्यानन्दशोकाद्यगोचरता, इत्यादीनि लिङ्गानि जीवन्मुक्तस्य ॥१९॥

19. The chief marks (Lingas) of a Jivanmukta are knowledge of the past, present and future, absolute fearlessness, absolute desireless, absolute painlessness, equal vision, balanced mind, freedom from exhilaration and depression, etc.

न जन्ममृत्यू न बन्धमोक्षौ न साधनसमाधी न ध्यातृध्येयौ न मुमुक्षुमुक्तौ इत्येतदेव पारमार्थिकं तत्त्वम् ॥२०॥

20. There is neither birth nor death, neither bondage nor freedom, neither Sadhana nor Samadhi, neither meditator nor meditated, neither seeker after liberation nor liberated—this is the ultimate truth.

Om Shanti! Om Shanti! Om Sahnti!

BASES OF VEDANTA

INTRODUCTION

The purpose of life is the realisation of one's own essential nature. It is to know that you are the pure ever-free Atman. The Vedanta expounds the great truth that Atman alone is real, the phenomenal world is unreal. You are Atman, but you forget your real Svarupa due to identification with the body. This is called Deha-Adhyasa. This is the greatest obstacle to Self-Knowledge or Atma-Jnana. To get over this delusion of identification with body the Vedantic Seers have made a detailed analysis of the different bodies, gross and subtle, and systematically proved that the Jiva is not the body but is identical with the Paramatman. The study of the three bodies, the five sheaths and the three states of waking, dream and deep sleep, helps man to understand that he is different from all these diverse modifications and that he is the unchanging, constant, witness of all these. This helps him to feel that he transcends the three states, the three bodies and the Panchakoshas.

Constant remembrance of this and meditation on this knowledge will lead him to the realisation of his Atma-svarupa. Therefore, the study of the Panchakoshas is a valuable aid in the process of dis-associating yourself from the bodies and the sheaths. It enables you to rise above body-consciousness, to feel that you are the Atman and thus remain quite unaffected and unattached amidst all distractions and tribulations of life.

I. THE THREE BODIES
THEIR ENUMERATION

(The individual experiencer is a consciousness-centre enveloped by several layers of matter existing as the factors causing objective awareness in it. The analysis of these layers or bodies is necessary to ascertain the nature of the true Self.)

Hari Om. Om Sat-Guru-Paramatmane Namah.

Disciple: How many bodies are there in an individual (Jiva)?

Guru: There are three bodies in every individual (Jiva).

Disciple: Please name them.

Guru: The physical body or the gross body (Sthula Sarira), the astral body or the subtle body (Sukshma Sarira or Lingadeha) and the causal body or the seed body (Karanasarira) are the three bodies.

Disciple: Please illustrate them.

Guru: The shell of a tamarind corresponds to the physical body. The pulp represents the subtle body. The seed corresponds to the causal body. Ice represents the physical body. H_2O represents the subtle body. The Tanmatras or root-elements correspond to the causal body.

THE GROSS BODY

Disciple: What are the components of the physical body?

Guru: The physical body is composed of five elements, viz., earth (Prithivi), water (Apah), fire (Tejas), air (Vayu) and space (Akasa).

Disciple: What are the seven primary essences (Sapta-Dhatus) of the physical body?

Guru: Chyle (Rasa), blood (Asra), flesh (Mamsa), fat (Medas), bone (Asthi), marrow (Majja) and semen (Sukla), are the seven primary essences of the physical body.

Disciple: What are the Shad-bhava-vikaras (six modifications of the body)?

Guru: Asti (existence), Jayate (birth), Vardhate (growth), Viparinamate (change), Apaksheeyate (decay), Vinashyate (death), are the six modifications or changes of the body.

Disciple: What are the links with which the body is connected?

Guru: The body (Deha), action (Karma), love and hate (Raga-dvesha), egoism (Ahamkara), non-discrimination (Aviveka) and ignorance (Ajnana) are the seven links of the chain of Samsara (world-experience). From Ajnana (ignorance), Aviveka is born. Aviveka is non-discrimination between the real and the unreal. From Aviveka is born Ahamkara or egoism; from egoism is born Raga-dvesha (like and dislike); from Raga-dvesha Karma (action) arises; from Karma the body or the Deha is produced. If you want to free yourself from the pain of birth and death, destroy ignorance (Ajnana), the root cause of this Samsara (world-experience), through the attainment of the Knowledge of Brahman or the Absolute. When ignorance is removed, all the other links will be broken by themselves. This physical body of yours is the result of your past actions and is the seat of your enjoyment of pleasure and pain.

Disciple: Why is the body called Sarira or Deha?

Guru: Because the body decays (Sheeryate) on account of old age, it is called Sarira. Because it is cremated or burnt (Dahyate) it is called Deha.

THE SUBTLE BODY

Disciple: What is the composition of the subtle body?

Guru: The subtle body is composed of nineteen principles (Tattvas), viz., five Jnana Indriyas or organs of knowledge, five Karma Indriyas or organs of action, five Pranas or vital airs, Manas or mind, Buddhi or intellect, Chitta or the subconscious and Ahamkara or the ego. It is a means of enjoying pleasure and pain.

Disciple: When will this subtle body get dissolved?

Guru: It gets dissolved in Videha Mukti or disembodied Liberation.

THE CAUSAL BODY

Disciple: What is the causal body (Karana Sarira)?

Guru: The beginningless ignorance that is indescribable is called the causal body. It is the cause of the gross and the subtle bodies.

Disciple: How can I transcend the three bodies?

Guru: Identify yourself with the All-pervading, Eternal Atman. Stand as a witness (Sakshi) of all experiences. Know that the Atman is always like a king—distinct from the body, organs, vital breaths, mind, intellect, ego and Prakriti—the Witness of their attributes.

II. THE FIVE SHEATHS

Disciple: What is meant by a Kosha?

Guru: Kosha means a sheath.

Disciple: Kindly illustrate these sheaths.

Guru: Just as a pillow-cover is a covering or a sheath for the pillow, just as a scabbard is a sheath for the sword or the dagger, so also this body, Pranas, mind, intellect and the causal body are sheaths that cover the Atman or the Soul.

There is the *singlet* close to the body; over this there is the shirt; over the shirt there is the waist-coat; over the

BASES OF VEDANTA 59

waist-coat there is the coat; over the coat there is the overcoat. Even so, the Atman is enveloped by these five sheaths.

Disciple: How many sheaths are there in the body?

Guru: There are five sheaths.

Disciple: Please name them.

Guru: Annamaya Kosha, Pranamaya Kosha, Manomaya Kosha, Vijnanamaya Kosha and Anandamaya Kosha are the five Koshas or sheaths.

Disciple: What is Annamaya Kosha?

Guru: Annamaya Kosha is food-sheath. It is the gross body made up of the five gross elements.

Disciple: Why is it called Annamaya Kosha?

Guru: It is called Annamaya Kosha, because it lives on account of food, it is made up of the essence of food, and, finally, it returns to food (earth or matter).

Disciple: What is Pranamaya Kosha?

Guru: Pranamaya Kosha is the vital sheath.

Disciple: What is the Pranamaya Kosha made of?

Guru: It is made up of the Pranas or the vital airs and the five Karmendriyas or organs of action.

Disciple: How many Pranas are there?

Guru: There are ten Pranas five Mukhya or chief Pranas, viz., Prana, Apana, Vyana, Udana and Samana, and five Upapranas or sub-Pranas viz., Naga, Kurma, Krikara, Devadatta and Dhananjaya.

Disciple: What is the function of Prana?

Guru: Ucchvasa and Nihshvasa (inhalation and exhalation) are the functions of the Prana.

Disciple: What is the function of Apana?

Guru: Excretion of faeces and urine is the function of the Apana.

Disciple: What is the function of Vyana?

Guru: Circulation of blood is the function of Vyana.

Disciple: What is the function of Udana?

Guru: Udana helps deglutition or swallowing of food. It takes the Jiva to rest in Brahman during deep sleep. It separates the astral body from the physical body at the time of death.

Disciple: What is the function of Samana?

Guru: Digestion of food is the function of Samana.

Disciple: What is the function of Naga?

Guru: Belching and hiccough or eructation and vomiting are the functions of Naga.

Disciple: What is the function of Kurma?

Guru: Closing and opening of eyelids are the functions of Kurma.

Disciple: What is the function of Krikara?

Guru: Causing of hunger is the function of Krikara.

Disciple: What is the function of Devadatta?

Guru: Yawning is the function of Devadatta.

Disciple: What is the function of Dhananjaya?

Guru: Nourishing the body, decomposition of the body after death and ejection of the child out of the womb in women are the functions of Dhananjaya.

Disciple: What are the two divisions in Prana?

Guru: Gross Prana and subtle Prana are the two divisions in Prana.

Disciple: What are the functions of these Pranas?

Guru: The gross Prana does the functions of breathing,

digestion, excretion, circulation, etc. The subtle Prana generates thought.

Disciple: What is Manomaya Kosha?

Guru: Manomaya Kosha is the mind-sheath.

Disciple: What does the mind-sheath consist of?

Guru: The mind-sheath consists of the mind (Manas), the subconscious (Chitta) and the five Jnanendriyas or the sense-organs of knowledge.

Disciple: What is Vijnanamaya Kosha?

Guru: It is the intellectual sheath.

Disciple: What does the intellectual sheath consist of?

Guru: It consists of the intellectual and the ego working with the help of the five Jnanendriyas or the sense-organs of knowledge.

Disciple: What is Anandamaya Kosha?

Guru: It is the bliss-sheath.

Disciple: Why is it called Anandamaya Kosha?

Guru: Because through it the Jiva or the individual soul experiences bliss during deep sleep and at the time of experiencing the effect of a Sattvic deed.

Disciple: What does the bliss-sheath consist of?

Guru: It is a modification of Prakriti and consists of the Vrittis called Priya, Moda and Pramoda.

Disciple: How many Koshas are in the physical body?

Guru: One Kosha—Annamaya Kosha..

Disciple: How many Koshas are in the Linga-shareera or subtle body (Astral body)?

Guru: Three sheaths, viz., Pranamaya, Manomaya, Vijnanamaya.

Disciple: How many sheaths are in the causal body or

Karana Sarira?

Guru: One sheath, viz., Anandamaya Kosha.

Disciple: How many sheaths operate during the waking state?

Guru: The five sheaths function during the waking state.

Disciple: How many sheaths function during the dream state?

Guru: Pranamaya, Manomaya, Vijnanamaya and Anandamaya Kosha function during dreaming state. Vijnanamaya and Anandamaya Kosha function partially.

Disciple: How many sheaths function during deep sleep?

Guru: Only one, viz., Anandamaya Kosha.

III. GUNAS

Disciple: What Guna is found in the physical body?

Guru: Tamoguna.

Disciple: What Guna is found in the Pranamaya Kosha?

Guru: Rajoguna.

Disciple: What is the Guna found in the Manomaya Kosha?

Guru: Sattva mixed with Tamas.

Disciple: What is the Guna found in the Vijnanamaya Kosha?

Guru: Sattva mixed with Rajas.

Disciple: What is the Guna found in the Anandamaya Kosha?

Guru: Sattva, technically called the Malina-Sattva (mixed with Rajas and Tamas) in contrast with

BASES OF VEDANTA

Suddha-Sattva of which Maya is the embodiment.

Disciple: Where are the Karmendriyas located?

Guru: In the Pranamaya Kosha.

Disciple: Where are the Jnanendriyas located?

Guru: In the Manomaya Kosha.

Disciple: Where does Jnanasakti rest?

Guru: In the Vijnanamaya Kosha.

Disciple: Where does Iccha Sakti rest?

Guru: In the Manomaya Kosha (mind).

Disciple: Where does Kriya Sakti rest?

Guru: In the Pranamaya Kosha.

Disciple: Please illustrate the function of Jnana Sakti, Iccha Sakti and Kriya Sakti.

Guru: You get knowledge of milk through intellect. You come to know that milk nourishes the body. This is the work of the Jnana Sakti of the Vijnanamaya Kosha. Then a desire arises in the mind to possess milk. This is the work of the Iccha Sakti or the Manomaya Kosha. Then you exert to obtain milk. This is the work of the Kriya Sakti of the Pranamaya Kosha.

Disciple: What are the attributes of the Anandamaya Kosha?

Guru: Priya, Moda, Pramoda.

Disciple: What is Priya?

Guru: The joy you experience when you look at an object you like.

Disciple: What is Moda?

Guru: The great joy you feel when you possess the object you like.

Disciple: What is Pramoda?

Guru: The greatest joy you experience after enjoyment of the object you like.

Disciple: What are the Vikaras (modifications) of the Annamaya Kosha?

Guru: Existence, birth, growth, change, decay and death.

Disciple: What are the Dharmas of the Pranamaya Kosha?

Guru: Hunger and thirst, heat and cold.

Disciple: What are the Vikaras of the Manomaya Kosha?

Guru: Sankalpa-Vikalpa (thinking and doubting), anger, lust, Harsha (exhilaration), Soka (depression) and Moha (delusion), etc. There are sixteen modifications of the Manomaya Kosha.

Disciple: What are the functions of the Vijnanamaya Kosha?

Guru: Discrimination and decision or determination (Viveka and Adhyavasaya or Nischaya), Kartritva and Bhoktritva (agency and enjoyership).

Disciple: What is the Dharma of the Anandamaya Kosha?

Guru: Experience of happiness.

Disciple: Please give the order of subtlety of the Koshas.

Guru: The Pranamaya Kosha is subtler than and pervades the Annamaya Kosha. The Manomaya Kosha is subtler than and pervades the Pranamaya and Annamaya Koshas. The Vijnanamaya Kosha is subtler than and pervades the Manomaya, the Pranamaya and the Annamaya Koshas. The Anandamaya Kosha is subtler than all the other four Koshas and pervades all of them.

IV. ADHYAROPA APAVADA

Disciple: What is the relation between the Kosha and the Atman?

Guru: Anyonya-Adhyasa.

Disciple: What is Anyonya-Adhyasa?

Guru: Anyonya-Adhyasa is mutual superimposition. The attributes of the five sheaths are superimposed on the Atman. The attributes of the sheaths, e.g, change pain, etc., are falsely attributed to the pure soul or the Atman. The attributes of the Pure Atman such as Existence, Knowledge, Bliss, Purity, Consciousness are transferred to the five sheaths.

Disciple: What is Adhyarpoa?

Guru: Adhyaropa is superimposition. Just as the snake is superimposed on the rope, the five Koshas are superimposed on the Atman.

Disciple: What is Apavadayukti?

Guru: It is sublation or negation of the five sheaths through "neti-neti" doctrine.

Disciple: What are the Shad Urmis?

Guru: Birth and death (for the physical body), hunger and thirst (for the Pranamaya Kosha), grief and delusion (Soka and Moha) for the Manomaya Kosha.

Disciple: Why are they called Urmis?

Guru: Just as there are waves in the ocean, these Shad Urmis are the waves in the ocean of this Samsara.

Disciple: How to develop the Vijnanamaya Kosha?

Guru: Through Viveka (discrimination), Vichara (enquiry), meditation on Atman, Japa of Omkara, etc.

Disciple: What will be the use of this purified and developed Vijnanamaya Kosha?

Guru: It will serve as a fortress to prevent coming in of sensual Samskaras from without and prevent the Samskaras of the Anandamaya Kosha or Karana Sarira from coming outside. It will help you to enter into profound meditation and Atma Vichara.

V. AVIDYA

Disciple: What is the cause of superimposition or Adhyasa?

Guru: Avidya or ignorance.

Disciple: What is the Adhara or Adhishthana for Avidya?

Guru: Brahman.

Disciple: How can Avidya remain in pure Brahman.

Guru: It is Anirvachaneeya. From the viewpoint of the Absolute there is neither Jiva nor Avidya nor the five sheaths. Avidya exists only for the Jiva.

Disciple: What is the other name for Avidya?

Guru: Anandamaya Kosha or Karanasarira of Jiva or individual soul.

Disciple: What does Avidya consist of?

Guru: It consists of Vasanas and Samskaras. The impression of the whole Sanchita Karma of all your past births are lodged there.

VI. THREE AVASTHAS

Disciple: What are the three Avasthas?

Guru: Jagrat Avastha (waking state), Svapna Avastha (dreaming state), Sushupti Avastha (deep sleep state).

Disciple: What is meant by Avastha?

Guru: Avastha means a state.

Disciple: What is Jagrat Avastha?

Guru: It is the state of waking consciousness. That state in which objects are known through the senses is known as Jagrat.

Disciple: What is Svapna Avastha?

Guru: That state in which objects are perceived through the impressions produced during waking state is called Svapna or dreaming state. The consciousness of the subtle, inner, subjective Prapancha or world, which during the quiescence of the sense-organs arises in the form of the percipient and object of perception by virtue of the latent impressions of what is seen and heard in Jagrat is Svapna.

Disciple: What is Sushupti?

Guru: That state in which there is total absence of knowledge of objects is deep sleep state. It is a remembrance in Jagrat state of the kind of experience, "I enjoyed sound sleep. I knew nothing."

VII. MOKSHA

Disciple: What is the nature of Moksha?

Guru: Sarvaduhkhanivritti (removal of all kinds of pain), and Paramanandaprapti (attainment of Supreme, imperishable, eternal Bliss of Brahman).

Disciple: What does Brahmajnana do?

Guru: It destroys Avidya and its effects (Karya), viz., the bodies and the whole Samsara. It frees you from the miseries of birth and death. It makes you absolutely fearless, free and independent. All your doubts like "whether I am body or Prana or Buddhi" will vanish in toto. You will become Anamaya, free from disease, old age and death. You will have no fear of death or enemies. You will shine as the effulgent, resplendent Purusha Supreme.

CATEGORIES IN VEDANTA

INTRODUCTION

The Prakriyas or the different categories in the Philosophy of Vedanta are the fundamental rudimentary principles with which its ethics and metaphysics are built up. They take into account both the Unmanifest and the manifest, Brahman, Maya, Isvara, Jiva and the universe. The nature of the Reality, the characteristics of the phenomenal appearance and the constitution of the individual self are the main themes of Vedantic discussion.

Sri Sankacharaya says that one must possess the fourfold qualification of Sadhana before entering into the study of Tattva-Bodha or the Knowledge of the Vedantic Categories and the Nature of the Atman. Sincere aspirants who have an ardent aspiration, faith, perseverance and purity of conscience will find a way of self-transformation through this knowledge. A thorough understanding of these different categories is necessary before starting to study the actual philosophy of the Advaita Vedanta which abounds with severe logic and penetrating reasoning over the eternal verities of existence.

THE CATEGORIES

1. There are twenty-four Tattvas or Principles of the manifestation of Mula Prakriti:

The five Tanmatras or rudimentary principles of the elements: Sabda (sound), Sparsha (touch), Rupa (form or colour), Rasa (taste), Gandha (smell).

The five Jnana-Indriyas or organs of perception: Shrotra (ear), Tvak (skin), Chakshus (eye), Jihva (tongue),

CATEGORIES IN VEDANTA

Ghrana (nose).

The five Karma-Indriyas or organs of action: Vak (speech), Pani (hand), Pada (feet), Upastha (genital), Payu (anus).

The five Pranas or vital forces: Prana, Apana, Samana, Udana, Vyana.

The fourfold Antahkarana or the internal organ: Manas (mind), Buddhi (intellect), Chitta (memory or subconscious), Ahamkara (egoism).

2. There are three bodies or Shariras: Sthoola-Sharira (gross physical body), Sukshma or Linga-Sharira (subtle body), Karana-Sharira (causal body).

3. There are five Koshas or sheaths covering the Jiva: Annamaya (food sheath), Pranamaya (vital sheath), Manomaya (mental sheath), Vijnanamaya (intellectual sheath), Anandamaya (bliss-sheath).

4. There are six Bhava-Vikaras or modifications of the body: Asti (existence), Jayate (birth), Vardhate (growth), Viparinamate (change), Apakshiyate (decay), Vinashyati (death).

5. There are five gross elements: Akasha (sky), Vayu (air), Agni (fire), Apah (water), Prithivi (earth).

6. There are five Upa-pranas or subsidiary vital airs: Naga, Kurma, Krikara, Devadatta, Dhananjaya.

7. There are six Urmis or waves (of the ocean of Samsara): Shoka (grief), Moha (confusion or delusion), Kshut (hunger), Pipasa (thirst), Jara (decay or old age), Mrityu (death).

8. There are six Vairis or enemies: Kama (passion), Krodha (anger), Lobha (greed), Moha (infatuation or delusion or confusion), Mada (pride), Matsarya (jealousy).

9. Maya is twofold: Vidya (knowledge), Avidya

(ignorance).

10. Vidya or knowledge is twofold: Para (higher), Apara (lower).

11. Avasthas or states of consciousness are three: Jagrat (waking), Svapna (dreaming), Sushupti (deep sleep).

12. Saktis are two: Avarana (veil), Vikshepa (distraction).

13. Jnana-Bhumikas or degrees of knowledge are seven: Subheccha, Vicharana, Tanumanasi, Sattvapatti, Asamsakti, Padarthabhavana, Turiya.

14. Ajnana-Bhumikas or degrees of ignorance are seven: Bija-Jagrat, Jagrat, Maha-Jagrat, Jagrat-Svapna, Svapna, Svapna-Jagrat, Sushupti.

15. Sadhana is fourfold: (a) Viveka (discrimination); (b) Vairagya (dispassion); (c) Shad-Sampat (six virtues) – (i) Shama (tranquillity of mind), (ii) Dama (self-restraint or control of the senses), (iii) Uparati (cessation from worldly activity), (iv) Titiksha (fortitude or power of endurance), (v) Shraddha (faith in God, Guru, Scriptures and Self), (vi) Samadhana (concentration or one-pointedness of mind); (d) Mumukshuttva (yearning for liberation).

16. The nature of Atman or Brahman is threefold: Sat (existence), Chit (consciousness), Ananda (bliss).

17. The Granthis or knots of the heart are three: Avidya (ignorance), Kama (desire), Karma (action).

18. The defects of the Jiva are three: Mala (impurity), Vikshepa (distraction), Avarana (veil of ignorance).

19. The Vrittis or modes of the mind are two: Vishayakara-Vritti (objective psychosis), Brahmakara-Vritti (Infinite Psychosis).

20. Gunas or qualities of Prakriti are three: Sattva (light and purity), Rajas (activity and passion), Tamas (darkness

CATEGORIES IN VEDANTA

and inertia).

21. The Puris or cities consisting the subtle body are eight: Jnana-Indriyas, Karma-Indriyas, Pranas, Antahkarana, Tanmatras, Avidya, Kama, Karma.

22. Karmas are three: Sanchita, Prarabdha, Agami.

23. The nature of a thing is fivefold: Asti, Bhati, Priya, Nama, Rupa.

24. Bhedas or differences are three: Svagata, Sajatiya, Vijatiya.

25. Lakshanas or definitions of the nature of Brahman are two: Svarupalakshana, Tatasthalakshana.

26. Dhatus or constituents of the body are seven: Rasa, (chyle), Asra (blood), Mamsa (flesh), Medas (fat), Asthi (bone), Majja (marrow), Shukla (semen).

27. There are four states of the Jnani: Brahmavit, Brahmavidvara, Brahmavidvariyan, Brahmavidvarishtha.

28. Anubandhas or matters of discussion (themes) in Vedanta are four: Adhikari (fit aspirant), Vishaya (subject), Sambandha (connection), Prayojyna (fruit or result).

29. Lingas or signs of a perfect exposition or a text are six: (i) Upakarma-Upasamhara-Ekavakyata: Unity of thought in the beginning as well as in the end; (ii) Abhyasa (reiteration or repetition); (iii) Apurvata (novelty or uncommon nature of the proof); (iv) Phala (fruit of the teaching); (v) Arthavada (eulogy, praise or persuasive expression); (vi) Upapatti or Yukti (illustration or reasoning).

30. Bhavanas or imaginations of the mind are three: Samshayabhavana (doubt), Asambhavana (feeling of impossibility), Viparitabhavana (perverted or wrong thinking).

31. Malas or impurities of the mind are thirteen: Raga, Dvesha, Kama, Krodha, Lobha, Moha, Mada, Matsarya,

Irshya, Asuya, Dambha, Darpa, Ahamkara.

32. Kleshas or worldly afflictions are five: Avidya, (ignorance), Asmita (egoism), Raga (love), Dvesha (hatred), Abhinivesha (clinging to body and earthly life).

33. Taapas or sufferings are three: Adhidaivika, Adhibhautika, Adhyatmika.

34. Pramanas or proofs of knowledge are six: Pratyaksha (perception), Anumana (inference), Upamana (comparison), Agama (scripture), Arthapatti (presumption), Anupalabdhi (non-apprehension).

35. Minds are two: Ashuddha (impure), Shuddha (pure).

36. Meditations are two: Saguna, Nirguna.

37. Muktas are two: Jivanmukta, Videhamukta.

38. Muktis are two: Krama-Mukti, Sadyo-Mukti.

39. Samadhis are two: Savikalpa, Nirvikalpa.

40. Jnana is twofold: Paroksha (indirect), Aparoksha (direct).

41. Prakriti is twofold: Para, Apara.

42. Apara Prakriti is eightfold: Earth, Water, Fire, Air, Ether, Mind, Intellect, Egoism.

43. Prasthanas or the regulated texts of Vedanta are three: Upanishads (Shruti), Brahmasutras (Nyaya), Bhagavad-Gita (Smriti).

44. There are two varieties of Granthas or Texts: Pramana-Granthas, Prameya-Granthas. The texts are again divided into two sections: Prakriya-Granthas and Shastra-Granthas.

45. Eshanas or desires are three: Daraishana (desire for wife), Vittishana (desire for wealth), Lokaishana (desire for this world and the other world).

CATEGORIES IN VEDANTA

46. Species of beings are four: Jarayuja (born of womb), Andaja (born of egg), Svedaja (born of sweat), Udbhijja (born of earth).

47. The sentinels to the door of salvation are four: Santi (peace), Santosha (contentment), Vichara (enquiry or ratiocination), Satsanga (company of the wise).

48. States of the mind are five: Kshipta (distracted), Mudha (dull), Vikshipta (slightly distracted), Ekagra (concentrated), Niruddha (inhibited).

49. Gates of the body are nine: Two ears, two eyes, mouth, nose, navel, genital, anus.

50. Avarana-Sakti is twofold: Asattva-Avarana, Abhana-Avarana.

51. Vikshepa-Sakti is threefold: Kriyasakti, Icchasakti, Jnanasakti.

52. Satta or existence is of three varieties: Paramarthika (absolutely real), Vyavaharika (phenomenal), Pratibhasika (apparent or illusory).

53. Knowledge is of two varieties: Svarupajnana (knowledge of the essential nature), Vrittijnana (psychological or intellectual knowledge).

54. Obstacles to Samadhi are four: Laya (torpidity), Vikshepa (distraction), Kashaya (attachment), Rasasvada (enjoyment of objective happiness).

55. The nature of the cosmic (Samashti) person (Isvara) is threefold: Virat, Hiranyagarbha, Isvara.

56. The nature of the individual (Vyashti) person (Jiva) is threefold: Vishva, Taijasa, Prajna.

57. Cognition is effected through two factors: Vritti-Vyapti (pervasion of the psychosis), Phala-Vyapti (pervasion of the result or consciousness).

58. The meaning of the Tat-Tvam-Asi Mahavakyas is

twofold: Vachyartha (literal meaning), Lakshyartha (indicative meaning).

59. Vedantic enquiry is practised through the methods of: Anvaya-Vyatireka, Atadvyavritti, Neti-neti doctrine, Adhyaropa-Apavada, Nyayas (illustrations), etc.

60. The meaning of the great dictum Tat-Tvam-Asi is ascertained through the considerations of Jahad-ajahallakshana or Bhagatyaga-lakshana, Samanadhikarana, Visheshanavisheshyabhava, Lakshya-lakshanasambandha.

61. The important Vadas in Vedanta are: Vivartavada, Ajativada, Drishti-Srishtivada, Srishti-Drishtivada, Avacchedavada, Pratibimbavada, Ekajivavada, Anekajivavada, Abhasavada.

62. Vedantic Contemplation is threefold: Sravana, Manana, Nididhyasana.

TAT TVAM ASI

That Thou Art

INTRODUCTION

'THAT THOU ART!' — Thus the Sruti emphatically and boldly voices forth the highest and most sublime truth that is the essence of all scriptures, nay, that is the goal of all scriptural teachings and assertions.

It is the greatest declaration ever made on the face of the earth. It is the profoundest teaching ever given since the dawn of creation. It is the only way of expressing and indicating the Truth that is beyond the reach of the mind and the senses. It is the one unique teaching that comforts the distressed humanity and infuses inner spiritual strength and courage into them to *pooh-pooh* the miseries and pains of mundane existence and soar high into the realm of non-dual, all-blissful eternal Existence.

If it be simple in the words that it employs, it requires the well-polished sharp intellect of the advanced aspirant to understand the subtlest Truth that it wishes to convey. If it be unostentatious in its expression, it is at once majestic and imperative in its utterance. If it be brief and blunt, aphoristic in its exposition of the highest Truth, it readily gets instilled deep in our hearts and minds, and from within us, it mysteriously raises our consciousness to that non-dual eternal plane of existence.

Such is the greatness of this Mahavakya, *Tat-Tvam-Asi*, which the Upanishadic Rishi, Uddalaka, employed to impart Brahma-Vidya to his son and disciple, Svetaketu.

THE MEANS TO REALISATION

Man is essentially Divine. He is not different from that eternal, non-dual substratum, Existence-Knowledge- Bliss Absolute. He is neither born into this Samsara, nor is he ever in a state of bondage. He is ever free, Nityamukta.

His present miseries and sufferings, his pains and limited pleasures, births and deaths, are all due to his erroneous identification with the five sheaths and the three bodies. And, in turn, this erroneous identification is the result of not-knowing of the truth, or the forgetfulness pertaining to it. This ignorance, Causal Ignorance, is at the root of all actions and reactions. Only the annihilation of this ignorance can lead us to our original state of non-dual blissful immortal existence.

This ignorance is not born of anything so that it can be destroyed through some action or other. It is simply a negative aspect. Just as absence of lights brings in darkness, absence of the sun brings in the night, so too, absence of Real Knowledge has brought in this Causal Ignorance.

No amount of fighting with darkness or night will destroy them. But, when the lamp or the sun is there, they disappear into nothingness, without leaving a trace. Similarly, where there is True Knowledge, there exists not even a trace of this Causal Ignorance. That True Knowledge is the Knowledge pertaining to our real, eternal, immortal Self which is not touched either by the causal ignorance or the effects of causal ignorance, just like the sun is not touched by the darkness of the night.

So, knowledge alone is the means for the Realisation of the Self; Self-Knowledge alone can liberate man from the meshes of Samsara.

TAT TVAM ASI

THE MAHA-VAKYAS

The scriptures, the Vedas and the Upanishads, exist to impart this Knowledge to all humanity so as to free them from this evanescent and ephemeral existence. Scriptural declarations can be grouped under three heads, viz.,—

Vidhi-Vakya or injunctions; Nishedha-Vakya or prohibitions; and Siddharthabodha-Vakya or the Maha-Vakya that proclaim the highest Truth, the identity of the Jivatman with the Paramatman, of the individual soul with the Supreme Soul.

The first two exist to purify the deluded Jiva and make him fit to understand and assimilate the third; for, only in a purified mind intuition will dawn, and with that alone can one attain the Highest Knowledge.

There are four Maha-Vakyas, each of the four Vedas containing one of them. The four Maha-Vakyas are:

Prajnanam Brahma:—'Consciousness is Brahman.' This is called the Svarupabodha-Vakya or the sentence that explains the nature of Brahman or the Self. This is contained in the Aitareya-Upanishad of the Rigveda.

Aham Brahma Asmi:—'I Am Brahman.' This is the Anusandhana-Vakya, the idea on which the aspirant tries to fix his mind. This is contained in the Brihadaranyaka Upanishad of the Yajurveda.

Tat Tvam Asi:—'That Thou Art.' This is the Upanishadic Vakya contained in the Chhandogya Upanishad of the Sama Veda. The teacher instructs through this sentence.

Ayam Atma Brahma:—'This Self is Brahman.' This is the Anubhavabodha Vakya or the sentence that gives expression to the inner intuitive experience of the aspirant. This is contained in the Mandukya Upanishad of the Atharva Veda.

Of these four Maha-Vakyas, *Tat Tvam Asi* is of great importance. It is the Upadesa-Vakya or Upanishad-Vakya. The Guru initiates the disciple into Brahma-Jnana only through this Vakya. This is also called Sravana-Vakya. This Maha-Vakya gives rise to the other three Vakyas.

The Guru instructs the disciple through *'Tat Tvam Asi,'* — Thou art That. The disciple hears it (Sravana), considers it deeply and reflects over the idea contained in it (Manana), meditates on that idea (Nididhyasana) and enters into Samadhi which leads to the Aparoksha Anubhuti, signified in the assertion *Aham Brahma Asmi*. To this experience, he gives expression through the Maha-Vakya *Ayam Atma Brahma,* and also asserts the nature or Svarupa of Brahman or the Self that he intuitively experiences through the Maha-Vakya *Prajnanam Brahma*.

The three words contained in this Vakya have got to be carefully analysed and understood. Through Sravana and Manana of the meaning of this Sentence, indirect knowledge or Paroksha-Jnana is had, and that is enough to destroy all sins. This Knowledge helps the aspirant to disown all actions and reactions, to renounce all attributes that he has taken upon himself in ignorance. He can lead a care-free, unperturbed and detached life in this world.

Nididhyasana and Samadhi give him the direct Knowledge or Aparoksha Jnana that frees him from causal ignorance which is the cause of the successive recurrence of births and deaths.

Therefore, it is essential to study this MahaVakya in all its details, word by word, taken separately and all together, and understand its meaning.

THE *A PRIORI* METHOD

Prakriti, the cause of ignorance, is made up of three Gunas, and carries with her the reflection of that transcendent Reality, Satchidananda. This Prakriti is divided into two aspects, called Maya and Avidya. Maya is Suddha-Sattva-Pradhana or that state of Prakriti in which the principle of Purity or Sattva, predominates over the other two, — Rajas and Tamas. Avidya is Malina-Sattva or that state of Prakriti in which Sattva is predominated and sullied by the other two.

When that pure Intelligence, Chit, is reflected through Maya or Suddha-Sattva, the reflected Consciousness is called Isvara. It is one only, and controls Maya. When that Chit is reflected in Malina-Sattva or Avidya, the reflected Consciousness is called Jiva. Due to the multifarious nature of Avidya, Jivas are too many, and being individualised and separated from one another, they are swayed by Avidya or ignorance. And this ignorance leads them to identification with the five sheaths and the three bodies. Thus, there is activity, pain and suffering for the Jiva.

In the sentence, *Tat Tvam Asi*, *Tat* refers to the reflected Consciousness in Maya and *Tvam* refers to the reflected Consciousness in Avidya. The word *Asi* proclaims their unity. It asserts that one Chit alone, reflected in a twofold way, goes under the names of Isvara and Jiva, when it is respectively qualified by the Upadhis of Maya and Avidya in its reflected State.

This, in short, is the *a priori* method of understanding the meaning of the Maha-Vakya, *Tat Tvam Asi,* the method arrived at from cause to effect.

THE STORY OF VIROCHANA

The foregoing analysis is not enough to convince an aspirant about his real nature and make him fix his mind in meditation upon the idea *'Aham Brahma Asmi'* — 'I am Brahman.' More often than not, men do misunderstand the real significance of the words employed to instruct them in

Brahma Vidya. It will be worthwhile to recollect the story of Virochana.

Once Indra and Virochana approached Prajapati to learn Atma Vidya. They underwent the rigorous discipline of discipleship for a period of thirty-two years. Thereafter Prajapati addressed them: "Look at yourselves in a cup of water and then whatever you do not understand about your Self, come and ask me."

After doing so they replied: "We see ourselves as we are."

Prajapati then asked them to adorn themselves with the best of clothes and look again in the water. They did so, and reported to Prajapati what they beheld of themselves. Hearing that Prajapati said: "That is the Self, the immortal Self."

They both went away to their respective abodes fully satisfied about the Vidya they had received. Prajapati said to Himself: "They both go away without having perceived and without having known the Truth or the Self, and whoever of these two, whether the Devas or the Asuras, will follow this doctrine will perish."

Virochana with a satisfied heart preached among his followers: The self (body) alone is to be worshipped, and so on. But Indra, before he returned to the Devas, experienced difficulty in getting convinced about the doctrine that the body is the Self. So he went back to Prajapati, and after a second period of thirty-two years' discipleship learnt that the dreaming self is the true Self. Being dissatisfied still, he was told that the self in sleep is the true Self, finally, after an austerity of one hundred and one years, he learnt that the real Self is above all individualistic implications.

The above story is not quoted without a purpose. Many

aspirants in the spiritual path have no patience to consider deeply the significance of the words employed to instruct them. As William Cobbett puts it, words are double-edged weapons. When properly understood, they will help one in all possible ways. When wrongly understood, they will be detrimental to one's progress. So, too, with the words *Tat, Tvam* and *Asi*. Their true significance can be well understood only after a long, detailed and careful consideration.

VACHYARTHA AND LAKSHYARTHA

The meaning of a word may be threefold. They are:

Vachyartha or primary meaning that is directly conveyed by the word; *Lakshyartha* or implied meaning or the meaning it conveys through implication; and *Vyangyartha* or suggested meaning, or the meaning hinted at or suggested by the word through its associations.

The relationship that exists between a word and its meaning is called Vritti. This Vritti is twofold, viz., Sakti Vritti and Lakshana Vritti.

That relationship which exists between a word and its meaning, and which has the power to generate Arthajnana or a knowledge of the meaning of the word is called Sakti Vritti. The meaning that is understood through the Sakti Vritti is called Vachyartha.

That Vritti which, with the help of the Vachyartha, is able to establish a long-standing relationship between the word and its meaning not directly expressed is called Lakshana Vritti. The meaning of a word that is understood with the help of the Lakshana Vritti is called the Lakshyartha.

This Lakshana Vritti is divisible into three groups, viz., Jahallakshana, Ajahallakshana and Jahadajahal- lakshana or Bhagatyaga Lakshana.

Jahallakshana: When the Vachyartha of a word is totally dispensed with and only the Lakshyartha is taken into account then it is called Jahallakshana. Jahat means 'to abandon.'

For example, consider the statement, *'Gangayam Ghoshah'* – 'In the Ganga there is the village of the cowherds.'

What the statement wishes to convey is not that the village is in the mid-stream or in the middle of the flowing river, but that the village is on the river bank. The direct meaning of the word 'Gangayam' (which denotes the actual flowing river) is totally abandoned and instead the implied meaning, 'Teere' (on the banks) is understood. The direct meaning refers to the river and the implied meaning to the bank. These two are totally different, one being water and the other earth. But, there exists a relationship between the river and the river banks.

Thus the Lakshana Vritti is that Vritti which generates the knowledge of a fit meaning (not directly had) in a word on the basis of the word's Vachyartha. And this new implied meaning bears a certain relationship to the Vachyartha, like the relationship between the river and the river banks.

Ajahallakshana: In this case, the Vachyartha is not abandoned but at the same time the Lakshyartha also is taken into account in combination with the Vachyartha.

Consider for example the statement, *'Sveto Dhavati'* – 'The White is running.'

Say, in a race-course someone is asking his neighbour which horse is running ahead. He may get the reply, 'The white is running.' It is known fully well that a colour cannot run. In this case the Lakshyartha of the word 'Svetah' is related to a horse. Therefore, it has got to be understood

TAT TVAM ASI

that a horse is running. But it is not enough if it is simply understood that 'a horse is running,' for it would not answer the question of the race-goer. So, the Vachyartha of the word Svetah (the white colour) is also retained, and the Lakshyartha, that is, 'the horse,' is combined with the Vachyartha, and the whole is understood together as 'the White horse is running.'

Jahadajahallakshana or **Bhagatyagalakshana:** In this we retain a certain portion or Amsa or Bhaga of the Vachyartha and discard the other portion.

Consider the statement: *'So(a)yam Devadattah'* – 'This is *that* Devadatta.'

A man saw Devadatta in the garb of a prince at Banaras. Ten years hence, he sees Devadatta in the garb of a Sannyasin at Rishikesh. It is natural for him to exclaim, "This is *that* Devadatta."

The word 'That' is associated with the idea of remoteness in space, and time, and of the garb of a prince. The word 'This' is associated with the idea of nearness in space and time, and of the garb of a Sannyasin. The Vachyartha of the word 'That' is a princely man who lived at Banaras ten years before. The Vachyartha conveyed by the use of the word 'This' is a Sannyasin living at Rishikesh at that particular time.

In the above statement certain things are contradictory and certain things are not. In that case we avoid or eliminate the contradicting factors. The Sannyasin and prince are contradictory. So too, Rishikesh and Banaras, and likewise, ten years before and ten years hence. In the statement 'This is That Devadatta,' we take only a portion of the Vachyartha of the two words 'This (Devadatta)' and 'That (Devadatta).' From the Vachyartha of the word 'That' we eliminate the garb of the prince, the place Banaras, and the time ten years before, but retain the person referred to.

So, too, in the Vachyartha of the word 'This' we retain the person referred to and eliminate the other three factors of space, time and appearance which contradict the first set. When this elimination and retention is done, then alone we can identify that Devadatta with this Devadatta.

This is also called *Lakshya-Lakshana-Bhava*. The words 'This' and 'That,' after the elimination of contrary association from their meanings, stand in the relation of the 'implier' and the implied (with Devadatta, the person who is common to both).

The sentence *'Tat Tvam Asi'* is to be understood only through the help of Bhagatyaga Lakshana.

BHAGATYAGA LAKSHANA

(As applied to *Tat Tvam Asi*)

In a foregoing context, while, concluding the details of the *a priori* method, it was said:

In the sentence *Tat Tvam Asi, Tat* refers to the reflected consciousness in Maya, and *Tvam* to the reflected consciousness in Avidya, the word *Asi* proclaiming their unity. It asserts that the one *Chit* alone, reflected in a twofold way, goes under the names Isvara and Jiva, when it is respectively qualified by the Upadhis Maya and Avidya in its reflected state.

Now, that conclusion is taken for consideration.

(A) *Vachyartha* of the word *Tat*:—

Tat refers to Isvara; He has the following qualifications and associations:

(1) Undifferentiated Maya is the space for the activities of Isvara.

(2) Creation, Maintenance and Destruction (Udhbhava, Sthiti and Samhara), are the three periods or Kala for

Isvara.

(3) Purity, Activity and Inertia (Sattva, Rajas and Tamas), are His means for creation, Srishti-Samagri.

N.B.: Maya and the three Gunas are one and the same thing. So there exists oneness between the space for Isvara's creation and Srishti Samagris. Of course, the body of Isvara is also to be included within that oneness. It is like this:

Earth becomes the space for the potter to do his work. Earth becomes the material for the potter to do his work. Lastly, earth itself, in the form of bones, etc., becomes the body of the potter. Thus is the unity of the three things.

(4) Virat, Hiranyagarbha and Avyakrita-Maya are three bodies of Isvara.

(5) Isvara in identification with the three is respectively called Vaisvanara, Sutratma and Antaryami.

(6) From the thought, 'I', the non-dual One, shall become many,' till the statement 'in the form of Jiva He entered,' all creation forms the Activity or Karya of Isvara.

(7) Omnipotence, Omniscience, Omnipresence, Being One only, Freedom (Svatantrya), Efficiency (Samarthya), Parokshattva (Remoteness), and the possessing of Maya as the limiting adjunct, — all the eight are the Dharmas of Isvara.

(8) (a) Maya in combination with all the eight categories referred to above; (b) Chidabhasa or the reflection of Chit contained in them; and (c) Brahman, the substratum for them — All of these go together to make up the Vachyartha of the word *Tat*.

To sum up, Maya and the rest (the gross, subtle and cosmic bodies) the Consciousness associated with Her and endowed with omniscience, rulership, etc., (by Consciousness Isvara, Hiranyagarbha and Vritti are meant here), and Pure eternal Consciousness not associated with any of the foregoing things, — when these three appear as an inseparable whole like a red-hot iron ball, they become the primary meaning of the word *Tat*.

(B) *Lakshyartha* of the word *Tat:*—

That Pure, unassociated Consciousness which remains after avoiding Maya and Her retinue and Chidabhasa, and which serves as the substratum of all these things, i.e., of the limiting adjuncts and of Isvara limited by them, becomes the implied meaning or Lakshyartha of the word *Tat*.

At this point, it will be worth one's while to note the mutual Adhyasa (the recognition of something previously observed in some other thing, this recognition being apparent and not real) that exists between Isvara and Brahman. This *Paraspara-Adhyasa* is born of non-discrimination. The Real, Eternal nature of Brahman is apparently recognised in Isvara. Hence, Isvara appears as real. Because the nature of Isvara and his creatorship are apparently recognised in Brahman, Brahman appears to be the cause of the Universe. Thus there is *Anyonya Adhyasa* between Brahman and Isvara, and this Adhyasa can be annihilated only through knowledge born of discrimination.

(C) *Vachyartha* of the word *Tvam:*—

Tvam refers to the individual Jiva with the following qualifications and associations:

(1) The eye, throat and the heart, — these three form the Desa or place for the Jiva.

(2) Jagrat, Svapna and Sushupti — Waking, Dreaming and Deep Sleep states, — these three form the three periods, Kala, or time for the Jiva.

(3) Sthula, Sukshma and Karana — Gross, Subtle and

TAT TVAM ASI

Causal, — are the three bodies for the Jiva.

(4) The above three themselves become the Bhoga-Samagri or the means of enjoyment for the Jiva.

(5) Visva, Taijasa and Prajna are the three names under which the Jiva goes in identification with the three bodies.

(6) The Samsara beginning from Jagrat and ending in Moksha becomes the Karya for the Jiva.

(7) Limited power and knowledge and limitation in space (the three things opposed to Omnipresence, etc.), multiplicity, being subservient (Paratantratva), absence of Samarthya (or strength), Aparokshatva (immediacy) and possession of Avidya or ignorance as the limiting adjunct, — these eight form the Dharma for the Jiva.

(8) Avidya associated with the above seven things, Chidabhasa, the reflection of Chit in Avidya, and Kutastha the substratum for both of them, — these three together become the Vachyartha for the word *Tvam*.

In short, individual ignorance or Avidya (including the three bodies), Consciousness (Visva, Taijasa and Prajna) associated with limited or partial knowledge, etc., and also the Pure Consciousness which is not associated with any of these attributes, — these three, when they appear as an inseparable whole like a red-hot iron ball, become the primary meaning of the word *Tvam*.

(D) *Lakshyartha* of the word *Tvam:*—

Kutastha who is the witness of the Jiva and who forms the substratum for the three bodies, etc., and who remains after avoiding the Chidabhasa combined with Avidya from the Vachyartha of the word *Tvam*, becomes the Lakshyartha for the word *Tvam*.

Like Brahman and Isvara, there exists mutual Adhyasa

between Kutastha and the Jiva. The reality of Kutastha is recognised in the Jiva and hence the Jiva appears to be real. Likewise, the nature of the Jiva and his Dharmas are recognised in Kutastha who is non-attached, non-doer, non-enjoyer and eternally free, and hence Kutastha appears in the opposite way. Thus the mutual Adhyasa between Kutastha and the Jiva. This can be annihilated only through Viveka-Jnana.

(E) *The inapplicability of Jahallakshana and Ajahallakshana:*

In Jahallakshana we avoid the whole of the Vachyartha. If we are to apply the Jahallakshana with reference to the two words *Tat* and *Tvam*, the following absurdities result, viz.,

1) The Pure Consciousness, Transcendent Brahman, included in the Vachyartha of the word '*Tat*' should be avoided, and,

2) as a result we shall have to take the insentient universe, or (by avoiding the entire universe along with the Pure Consciousness) we shall have to take only Sunyata or Voidness.

Because of these two, only disaster will result and Moksha cannot be attained.

In Ajahallakshana we do not avoid any part of the Vachyartha but take the entire meaning. In doing so, while retaining the full Vachyartha, for the Lakshyartha portion we shall have to take again only Sunyata. It does not help us in any way towards our goal. Thus both Jahallakshana and Ajahallakshana are inapplicable in the case of the Maha-Vakya, *Tat Tvam Asi.*

In Bhagatyaga-Lakshana we avoid the contradicting portions but retain the non-contradicting portion. In applying this in the case of the two words, *Tat* and *Tvam*,

(1) we avoid Maya and Avidya, the portions that contradict, from the respective Vachyarthas, and

(2) retain the Pure Consciousness that is non-contradicting.

Hence there exists a means for the goal.

So, Bhagatyaga-Lakshana alone is admissible in the case of the Maha-Vakya *Tat Tvam Asi*.

THE IDENTITY BETWEEN *TAT* AND *TVAM*

In discussing the Bhagatyaga Lakshana, it was observed that Isvara and Brahman, and Jiva and Kutastha, respectively become the Vachyartha and Lakshyartha of the two words *Tat* and *Tvam*. Now it is proposed to establish the unity that exists between the two Lakshyarthas, that is, between Kutastha and Brahman.

Both of them refer to unassociated Pure Consciousness. Both of them are of the nature of Pure Consciousness. Consciousness is Consciousness wherever it be. Therefore, they are identical. That identity can be explained through the following examples:

There is difference between Ghatakasa (ether in a pot) and Mahakasa (ether in the vast expanse outside). The difference in this case is not born out of any difference in the quality of the ether present in the pot and in the vast space outside. Ether is the same everywhere. The difference is solely born out of the angle of vision. When the angle of vision is directed from the limiting adjunct, the pot, and fixed upon the ether, then the difference between Ghatakasa and Mahakasa ceases to exist, and oneness alone is seen.

Likewise, difference exists between Ganga water that flows in the river and the Ganga water that is stored up in a small pot. One can talk about the river water and the pot water when one's angle of vision is directed towards the container. But, when the water, i.e., the contained, is considered in itself, in both the cases it is water and water alone that cannot be differentiated.

Similarly with an oil lamp made of clay and another made of glass. There definitely exists a difference between the two lamps. But the flame is identical when considered in its nature as fire.

The same man is addressed as the father and the son respectively by his son and his father. Being the son and being the father are two different things. This difference exists when he is respectively qualified by the relation that he bears to his son and the relation that he bears to his father. But, his nature of being a man is not affected by either of the two relationships or attributes. Considered by himself, he is a man, and man alone.

Such is the identity, the oneness, that exists between Kutastha (the Lakshyartha of the word *Tvam*) and Brahman (the Lakshyartha of the word *Tat*). Thus the identity between the two words *Tat* and *Tvam* is established by the help of the Bhagatyaga Lakshana.

This method of establishing the identity between Kutastha and Brahman is technically called *Mukhya-Samanadhikarana*. There is the other type of Samanadhikarana which goes under the name *Badha-Samanadhikarana*. This helps us to establish the identity between Jiva and Brahman.

In this case we negate the attributes and limiting adjuncts of one of the two given things, and identify the remaining (non-negated) portion with the second thing through Mukhya-Samanadhikarana.

Here, to establish the identity between Jiva and Brahman, first we negate the limiting between Jiva and Upadhis of the Jiva and then identify the Pure

TAT TVAM ASI

Consciousness left over with Brahman. This is like establishing the relationship between Jalakasa (space reflected in water) and Mahakasa (space external to water).

INAPPLICABILITY OF VISESHANA VISESHYA BHAVA

It is open for anyone to contend that the words *Tat* and *Tvam* may be interpreted and identified through the use of either solely Samanadhikarana or Viseshana Viseshya Bhava as in the case of a *Blue Lotus,* without the help of Bhagatyaga Lakshana. The answer to that is that the literal meaning, as understood in the statement 'the blue lotus,' does not fit in with the sentence *Tat Tvam Asi.*

In the assertion 'the blue lotus,' the two words 'blue' and 'lotus,' by themselves, are two contrary ideas, but still they qualify each other so as to signify a common object. This mutual qualification is Viseshana Viseshya Bhava.

All lotuses are not blue and all blue things are not lotuses. But in this particular case, *blue* qualifies the word lotus and *lotus* qualifies the word blue. Thus they qualify each other and there exists a mutual qualifier-qualified relationship. Thus, temporarily avoiding all their distinctions, they unite together to mean that thing which we call the blue lotus, the Samanadhikarana.

This type of interpretation cannot be given to the sentence *'Tat Tvam Asi.'*

In the statement 'the blue lotus,' though the word 'blue' and 'lotus' are two contrary ideas, yet, they exist on one and the same substratum, Samanadhikarana, and further stand in the mutual relationship of qualifier and qualified to denote a common basis.

In the case of *Tat* and *Tvam,* they are two contrary ideas respectively associated with remoteness and nearness. As such, their co-existence in one and the same individual is not possible. Further, it cannot be argued that after eliminating their mutual distinctions they stand in the mutual relationship of the qualifier and the qualified, on the same substratum, so as to mean that substratum.

In the sentence *Tat Tvam Asi* there is no effort to bring two contrary ideas in the relationship of the qualifier and the qualified, and thus to effect a unity between two contrary ideas, so as to bring out the meaning of the substratum. The true significance of the sentence *Tat Tvam Asi* is an absolute homogeneous Consciousness.

The inadmissibility of Jahallakshana and Ajahallakshana were discussed before. Now the inadmissibility of Samanadhikarana and Viseshana Viseshya Bhava have been discussed.

Thus, Bhagatyaga Lakshana or Jahadajahallakshana alone is admissible in getting at the true meaning of the sentence *Tat Tvam Asi.*

REALISATION

When the true significance of the words *Tat* and *Tvam* are heard and considered through the method of refutation of superimposition and identification of the Consciousness, there arises in the mind of the aspirant an idea pertaining to that state of Absolute Oneness. There is a perfect and unswerving idea and feeling in the aspirant that he himself is Brahman. *'Aham Brahma Asmi'* (I am Brahman), he feels He meditates over that idea continuously and enters the state of Samadhi and Self-realisation.

Now, it may be asked as to whom this Knowledge comes, whether to the Kutastha or the Chidabhasa.

Primarily, this knowledge dawns in Chidabhasa. The Chidabhasa who is associated with the Buddhi or intellect, firstly negates his Svarupa as such. Because of this negation, he knows himself as the Kutastha who is the Lakshyartha of the word *'Aham'* (I). When once he knows himself to be Kutastha, there is no difficulty for him to know that he is Brahman, for, verily, Kutastha Himself is Brahman.

RIGHT SIGNIFICANCE OF 'TAT TVAM ASI'

A Mahavakya in an Upanishad is a transcendental phrase or a great saying which establishes identity or oneness of the individual soul with Brahman. There are altogether four Mahavakyas in the Upanishads. Each Veda contains one Mahavakya. The four Mahavakyas are:—

1. *Prajnanam Brahma* (Consciousness is Brahman): This is contained in the Aitareya Upanishad of the Rigveda. This is the Svarupa-Bodha-Vakya that explains the nature of Brahman or the Self.

2. *Aham Brahmasmi* (I am Brahman): This is contained in the Brihadaranyaka Upanishad of the Yajur Veda. This is the Anusandhana-Vakya or sentence for enquiry.

3. *Tat Tvam Asi* (That Thou Art): This is contained in the Chhandogya Upanishad of Sama Veda. This is Upadesha Vakya uttered by the Guru to disciple.

4. *Ayam Atma Brahma* (This Atman is Brahman): This is contained in the Mandukya Upanishad of the Atharva Veda. This is the Anubhava-Bodha-Vakya that gives expression to the inner intuitive experience of the innermost Self by the aspirant through meditation or Nididhyasana.

Out of the four Mahavakyas we are concerned here with the Upadesha Vakya *"Tat Tvam Asi"* for "Pada-Artha-Sodhana" or an examination into the real meaning of it.

In the Chhandogya Upanishad it is stated that the sage Uddalaka sends his son Svetaketu to Gurukula for learning the Vedas. Svetaketu accordingly spends twelve full years in learning the scriptures and thus returns home with the vanity of being learned. His father asks him: "My dear, why

(93)

are you so conceited? Have you learnt that, by learning which the unheard becomes heard, the unknown becomes known, the unperceived becomes perceived."

"How is it?" asks Svetaketu, and the father gives the reply: "It is just as by knowing one clod of clay all that is made of clay is known: for whatever the modifications of the effects are, they are only names, and have their origin in speech. One who knows the cause knows all its effects, since the cause and its effects are non-different." Then Uddalaka gives various examples for ascertaining the cause of the universe. His instructions may be summed up as follows:

1. The effect is nothing but the cause. Hence the body is nothing but food, food is nothing but water, water is nothing but fire, fire is nothing but *Sat*. *Sat* alone is true, and *That thou art*.

2. When a man sleeps he becomes one with *Sat* and hence in his case it is said *Svapiti,* which means *he attains his own Self* in sleep. This *Sat* is the real cause of the universe.

3. When a man dies his speech is dissolved in the mind, the mind is dissolved in the Prana, the Prana is dissolved in fire, fire is dissolved in *Sat*. This *Sat* is thy Self — *That thou art.*

Sage Uddalaka gives nine examples and repeats the Mahavakya *"Tat Tvam Asi,"* with each of them, to bring home to Svetaketu the real significance of the great sentence. Evidently the qualifying pronoun *"That"* refers to *"Sat"* or God, the creator, and *"Thou"* refers to the individual soul. *"Art"* or *"Asi"* connects them both, indicating thus an identity between the two, which is the subject matter of consideration in this present essay.

Objection 1: But in what way can Godhood be

RIGHT SIGNIFICANCE OF 'TAT TVAM ASI'

attributed to an individual? They both have antagonistic qualities. They can never be identical. But as Vishnu is read in an image, or as Aditya, Agni, etc., are worshipped as Brahman, in the same way Godhood can be attributed to the Jiva.

Reply: — No, it cannot be. *'Tat Tvam Asi'* has a totally different signification. The word 'etc' in the above objection signifies that Aditya, Agni, and the like are not themselves Brahman. Similarly an image itself is not Brahman. But this is not the case with the Mahavakya.

Objection 2: — This may be used in the case of *Stuti* or glorification, just as it is said: thou art Indra, Varuna etc.

Reply: — No, Svetaketu cannot be glorified by his father, who is superior to him in position and knowledge.

Objection 3: — It may be used in a secondary sense, just as someone may say: 'Thou art a lion,' meaning thereby 'thou art as brave as a lion.'

Reply: Secondary sense has no place here since the instruction of Uddalaka is on the knowledge of the cause, vide for example, *"as by knowing a clod of earth one can know all its effects..."*

Objection 4: — If Svetaketu is *Sat*, there is no necessity of knowing himself, and the instruction is of no avail.

Reply: — No; due to illusory identification with the body, mind, etc., the Self which is *Sat* is not known. When the illusion vanishes, *Sat* shines by its own light. The instruction that the unheard becomes heard etc. signifies that *Sat* is not known by the senses and the intellect. On the other hand it is known by direct perception or intuition. Thus we proceed with our enquiry into the real meaning of *'Tat Tvam Asi'* which establishes non-duality, cutting off the tree of Samsara.

SAMANADHIKARANYA

This is the relation of abiding in a common substratum, as for instance, the ether in a pot (Ghata) and the ether in a temple (Matha) have a common substratum. Being limited by pot and temple they differ apparently; yet by negating the limiting adjuncts, viz., the pot and the temple, we find the same ether undifferentiated.

Pot-ether (Ghatakasa) is not equal to Temple-ether (Mathakasa). But, Pot-ether minus Pot is equal to Temple-ether minus Temple. Ether is equal to Ether.

This is the case of Samanadhikaranya. The same holds good in the case of 'Tat' and 'Tvam,' which we will prove by considering their indicative meaning.

In order to know the meaning of a sentence one must know the meaning of each 'Pada' or word. Every word is related to its meaning. This relationship is called exposition or Vritti.

There are two Vrittis:—

(1) Sakti-Vritti (Force) (2) Lakshana-Vritti (indication)

Sakti Vritti:— It is the potency inherent in the word by which one is able to know its meaning. When the word *Jar* is uttered, one is able to know the roundness, its neck, etc., only by its Sakti-Vritti. But one word may have different interpretations according as they are used in different circumstances. This further specification of Sakti-Vritti by which we ascertain a possible meaning is called 'Sakya' or 'Possible.' The meaning thus ascertained is called 'Sakyartha' or 'Vachyartha.' As, for example, in the Mahavakya *'Tat tvam asi'* we are not concerned with all the individual cases of 'Tat' and 'Tvam.' Here these are adjectival pronouns qualifying God and Jiva. We mean by them God and Jiva respectively. Hence "Vachyartha" or "Sakyartha" of "Tat" is God and that of "Tvam" is 'Jiva.'

RIGHT SIGNIFICANCE OF 'TAT TVAM ASI'

Without the knowledge of Vachyartha (possible meaning of a term) no knowledge of indication is produced.

Lakshana Vritti:— That which indicates or distinguishes a word is called indication. It is of three varieties:

(1) Jahat-Lakshana, (2) Ajahat-Lakshana and (3) Bhagatyaga-Lakshana.

(1) *Jahat-Lakshana* (non-inclusive indication): In the sentence, "There is a village in the Ganga," if we take the Vachyartha of Ganga, we cannot make out the sense of the sentence, since a village can never be situated in the Ganga. But if we abandon the literal meaning of the word *Ganga* and make it to signify its bank, then the sentence has a correct meaning. Hence the Jahat-Lakshana of the Pada "Ganga" is its bank. Thus in Jahat-Lakshana the whole of the Vachyartha is abandoned and it (Vachyartha) is made to indicate a totally different thing.

(2) *Ajahat-Lakshana* (inclusive indication): In the sentence, "The white is galloping," we can make out the meaning of the sentence by introducing a word 'horse' into it and thus meaning 'The white horse is galloping.' The word 'white' indicates a larger sense. Here the Ajahat-Lakshana of the word 'white' is horse. Thus in Ajahat-Lakshana the whole of the Vachyartha is retained and something more is included into it.

(3) *Bhaga-Tyaga-Lakshana* or *Jahadajahat-Lakshana* (indication abiding in the one part of the meaning while the other part of it is abandoned):

This is the combination of *Jahat* and *Ajahat,* which mean, literally, *leave* and *take,* respectively. A portion of the Vachyartha is left out, and a portion of it is taken.

As, for instance, when a thing seen in a prior period is found subsequently in another place, a person is apt to say

"That is This." A person named Devadatta, for example, seen a few years back in Calcutta may be seen today in Rishikesh, and thus we may recognise him by saying: "That is this Devadatta." Here "That" refers to a thing seen in the past time, and in another place, and "This" conveys the sense of the present time at the present moment. Hence two adjectival pronouns referring to the past and the present apply contradictions. Therefore, by abandoning the indications of 'That' and 'This' the apparent inconsistency is removed, and as both of them refer to the same substance, their equality is identity.

To put it algebraically we have to equate:

That is not equal to This.

Considering "Vachyartha" of both the words, we find:

Dedavatta plus Past time is not equal to Devadatta plus Present time. Applying Bhagatyaga in both the terms:

Devadatta is equal to Devadatta. Thus Bhagatyaga-Lakshana of "That" Pada is Devadatta, and that of "This" Pada also is Devadatta. The equality is that of identity.

Now let us proceed to consider as to which of the Lakshanas is applicable in the case of "Tat tvam" Pada.

1. *JAHAT-LAKSHANA IS INAPPLICABLE*:

The conclusion of Vedanta with reference to the signification of 'That' and 'Thou' is to establish the non-duality or identity of the witnessing intelligence of the individual with the Universal or Brahman-intelligence. Hence both the Padas, 'Tat' and 'Tvam' contain within themselves, 'Brahman' and 'Atman,' respectively.

If Jahat-Lakshana is applied in construing the sentence, their Vachyartha will be completely abandoned and another object will be introduced as what is to be

RIGHT SIGNIFICANCE OF 'TAT TVAM ASI'

known. This another object must be devoid of intelligence and hence the purpose of the Mahavakya remains unserved.

2. AJAHAT-LAKSHANA IS INAPPLICABLE:

In Ajahat-Lakshana, the literal meaning is wholly retained and something more is introduced into it. If the Vachyartha of 'Tat' and 'Tvam,' i.e., 'God' and 'Jiva' is retained, both being totally different, such signification is contradictory. Thus Ajahat-Lakshana, too, is inapplicable in the case of the Mahavakya.

3. BHAGA-TYAGA-LAKSHANA IS APPLICABLE:

According to Abhasavada, Maya, the reflected shadow of intelligence in Maya, and the abiding intelligence of Maya, is Isvara, with the attributes of Omnipotence, Omniscience and the rest, and that is indicated by the word "Tat". The reflected shadow of intelligence in the distributive aggregates of ignorance as well as its abiding intelligence, is Jiva, with the attributes of finiteness, little-knowingness, etc., and this is indicated by the word "Tvam". By applying Bhaga-Tyaga-Lakshana, we will have to abandon a part from each of the Padas, "Tat" and "Tvam". Thus the Lakshyartha of "Tat" is Brahman or intelligence which is found by removing the Upadhi (Maya), Upadhi Dharma and Abhasa Chaitanya from its Vachyartha, "Isvara". Similarly the Lakshyartha of "Tvam" is Kutastha or witnessing intelligence which is found by removing Upadhi (Avidya), Upadhi-Dharma, and Abhasa-chaitanya from its Vachyartha, "Jiva".

We have to equate:

TAT = TVAM
Applying Bhagatyaga

(God – Upadhi & Upadhi Dharma & Abhasa Chaitanya)
= (Jiva – Upadhi & Upadhi Dharma & Abhasa Chaitanya)

Therefore Lakshyartha:

Chidakasa = Kutastha or Pervading intelligence = Witnessing intelligence or Intelligence = Intelligence.

In the same way we can apply Bhagatyaga-Lakshana from the standpoint of Bimba-Pratibimba-Vada, Karya-Karana-Upadhi-Vada, Avachhinna-Anvachhinnavada and Avachhedavada.

In each case the non-duality of the supreme Self and the individual self is proved. Thus we have seen that Bhagatyaga-Lakshana alone is applicable. To make it clear we may take recourse to either of the following ways:—

1. Vachyartha of Tat and Vachyartha of Tvam.

2. Lakshyartha of Tat and Vachyartha of Tvam.

3. Vachyartha of Tat and Lakshyartha of Tvam.

4. Lakshyartha of Tat and Lakshyartha of Tvam.

All the former three cases are clearly absurd. Only the last case is applicable in serving the purpose.

THE METHOD OF CONNECTION

It has been already proved that 'Tat' Pada indicates the witnessing intelligence. In their Vachyarthas, 'Tat' Pada is marked by the mistaken conception of indirectness (Parokshata-Bhranti) and 'Tvam' Pada is marked by finitude or (Parichhinnata-Bhranti). To remove these two misconceptions in their Lakshyarthas we should say: 'Tat-Tvam' marking the significance of 'Tat,'—subject and 'Tvam'—predicate. This removes the first Bhranti, i.e., the misconception of indirectness pertaining to the significance of the Pada 'Tat.' That is to say 'Chidakasa or Brahman is Kutastha.' This gives direct perception, removing the misconception of the indirectness of Chidakasa.

In the same way if we say 'Tvam Tat' we remove the misconception of finitude pertaining to Tvam Pada. Here

RIGHT SIGNIFICANCE OF 'TAT TVAM ASI'

the significance of 'Tvam' is subject and significance of 'Tat' is predicate. That is to say, 'Kutastha' is 'Chidakasa.' Thus the misconception of finitude pertaining to Kutastha is removed. This, in short, is the examination in the real significance of 'Tat Tvam Asi.' One who meditates upon it, comes to know that he is not the body, not the mind, is neither doer nor enjoyer, but he is Existence, Knowledge and Bliss Absolute. He becomes full of Bliss by sacrificing the miseries of the world and attains the real nature, i.e. Brahman.

The initiation into the mysteries of 'Tat Tvam Asi' by a Brahmanishtha Guru alone can enable one to know the correct significance of the Mahavakya which destroys Samsara in the same way as the sun dispels darkness.

1. MEANS TO REALISATION

THE GOAL OF LIFE is Self-realisation. It is not the attainment of anything external to us, but it consists in our simply knowing or becoming aware of our eternally Free nature. If it were an impossibility to get convinced that we are Existence-Absolute and eternally Free, why should the Srutis repeatedly teach us that doctrine like an affectionate mother? On the other hand that doctrine contradicts not but asserts our own inner urge, 'Let me ever live in a blissful state free from all pain and misery.'

How the idea of a snake is negated from a rope-snake, so too, the non-Self is negated from the Self that is eternally existing. That is done through reasoning on the evidence of Sruti passages like, 'Tat Tvam Asi' etc. With the dawn of true knowledge, the Self-luminous Self alone shines and the non-self totally disappears into an airy nothing like the disappearance of the snake when the rope is known as such with the aid of a lamp.

Is there a means that can be handled by the aspirant

to attain realisation? Are injunctions and prohibitions on Vedic lines applicable to the seeker after Truth?

To put it in a nut-shell, the seeker after Truth cannot be subjected to Vedic injunctions and prohibitions.

The injunctive side of the Scriptures merely restates popular conceptions and beliefs when it says 'do this,' 'Thou art the doer and enjoyer' etc. It points out to a certain object for our attainment. The injunctions and prohibitions are made with sole reference to the object that has got to be attained. Hence, in that case, injunctions and prohibitions are justified.

In all Vedanta (i.e., the Upanishads), nowhere do we find a clear mention of the Self as the object to be attained. The only way by which the Upanishads point the Truth is through the words. 'Neti, Neti.' The Self is never an object for our attainment. Sruti passages like 'Tat Tvam Asi' proclaim the Truth or give us the right Knowledge from the transcendent level, Paramarthic standpoint. They do not, however, point out an *object* for our attainment. Further, the knowledge arising out of injunctive scriptures gets contradicted by the knowledge arising out of Sruti passages like, 'Tat Tvam Asi.'

Of the two ideas, 'I am Existence-Absolute,' and 'I am the experiencer,' both of which have the Immortal Self as the Witness, the latter which owes its origin to ignorance and which springs up from apparent evidences like sense-perception gets negated from the implied meaning (Lakshyartha) of the word 'I' (the implied meaning of 'I' is represented by the former) on the authority of the Sruti passages like, 'Tat Tvam Asi.'

REASONING AND REITERATION AS MEANS

Some hold that one does not attain Absolute Liberation on hearing the words 'Tat Tvam Asi' or by knowing the

RIGHT SIGNIFICANCE OF 'TAT TVAM ASI'

literal meaning of the Maha Vakya without reiteration and reasoning. Hence they wish to enjoin these two things as essential means to the seeker after truth. They contend that on the absence of scriptural injunctions, our conduct should be deemed as non-scriptural which position is not desirable. According to them, the result 'Thou Art That' being stated as the end to be achieved, austerities, self-control, renunciation of things incompatible with that end, reiteration and reasoning should necessarily be accepted as the means enjoined for the attainment of that result.

It has been already stated that injunctions can be accepted provided the Upanishads particularise and define the end to be achieved. But, the Upanishads end with 'Neti, Neti.' The sentence 'Tat Tvam Asi' is not stated as a result to be attained through certain actions; the sentence proclaims the Truth. Therefore, even reiteration and reasoning cannot be enjoined as means to an end to the seeker of Truth.

THE ACTUAL POSITION

The superimposition of the ego on the eternally Free Self and transferring the ego's actions and experiences to the actionless Self is akin to the father's superimposing of the son's distress upon himself (upon the father) whereas, in truth, he (the father) has none. While stating 'Neti, Neti,' the scriptures do negate the superimposition as if that superimposition were a reality. Injunctions, reiteration, etc., are all due to that superimposition. While the superimposition which has no real existence by itself is negated, how can injunctions, reiteration, etc., be sustained? Are they not negated along with the superimposition? So, taiking of injunctions when they are negated is not reasonable.

The negation of the ego from the Self is like the

de-superimposition of the superimposed (in ignorance) colour from the sky by the ignorant people. This negation is not of a real thing. If real things were to be negated, then, surely, liberation would become transitory.

A certain amount of reiteration and reasoning is necessary to grasp the truth contained in the Sruti passage like 'Tat Tvam Asi' and to get firmly convinced of the same to the point of experience. But they cannot be construed to be injunctions on the lines of the Vedic ones. They help us to deny perceptional knowledge that is more powerful than inferential knowledge, and to strengthen our faith in the inferential knowledge. They help us to negate ignorance, but, they do not directly and positively present us with Self-knowledge as a result of their being put to use as a means.

Self is Svayam-Prabha. It shines by Its own Light. It is known by Its Own Self. In the strict sense, there exists no means to realise the Self.

To a coward who doubts whether he exists or not what means can one suggest so that his (the coward's) existence can be 'attained' by him (the coward?).

2. EGO AND THE SELF

On account of its proximity to the Self, the ego appears to be conscious. Hence the two ideas or words 'I' and 'Mine' originate. As the ego is possessed of genus, action, etc., words are applicable to it. But words cannot be applied to the Self that is actionless and that is not an object for any word to point out or signify it. A word or idea can only be applied to *objects* of knowledge and not to non-objects. So, Brahman or Self is not within the scope of any word or an idea.

Words that denote the ego and all the other things that reflect the Self only indirectly express the Self and by no means describe it directly. Similar to the application of words that denote the action of fire (e.g., burning) in an indirect way (never directly) to the torch etc. (e.g., the torch burns), words implying the Self (the word 'I' implying Existence, etc.) are applied to the ego which has the reflection of the Self in it, and further, appears to be like the Self.

EXAMPLE OF THE REFLECTION OF A FACE IN A MIRROR

The reflection of a face in a mirror is different from the face; the reflection imitates the mirror inasmuch as it possesses the property of being in the mirror and the quality of the mirror. The reflection depends on the mirror for its existence. But the real face does not. So, the real face is different from the reflection. Similarly, the reflection of the Self in the ego is different from the Pure Self.

In the case of the face, the face is real but not its reflection in the mirror. The reflection is not always there. But, at the same time, the reflection is not totally unreal since it is seen at times. Hence, the reflection is indescribable and the face is different from it. In the case of the Pure Self and Its reflection, in fact, however, both of them are devoid of any real distinction. In the case of the face and the mirror, the mirror has an existence independent of the face. But, in the case of the Pure Self, the intellect which is the reflecting medium is not having an independent existence all by itself, apart from the existence of the Pure Self. Therefore, the distinction between the Pure Self and Its reflection is only apparent and not real. Owing to a non-discrimination due to ignorance between the Pure Self and Its reflection, the Self is regarded as an individual suffering transmigratory existence.

It may be said that the reflection of the Self in the ego, as distinct from the Pure Self, is the individual soul experiencing and acting in this universe, on the authority that the individual soul is a real entity having its own properties like the shadow of a tree having the property of refreshing any one coming under it on a hot midday. That cannot be so. The refreshing property cannot be attributed to the shadow, for it is the effect of refraining from the warm things, say, the hot sun. Further, because of that, it cannot be said that the refreshing property that is seen in the shadow is ample proof for accepting the reality of the shadow. One is not refreshed by sitting close to a burning hearth under its shadow.

The reflection of the face in the mirror is neither the property of the face nor the property of the mirror. If it were the property of either of the two, then, it should continue to exist when one of the two is not there. If it can be said that the reflection is the property of both the real face and the mirror, it can be equally refuted by saying that even when both the mirror and the face are there but improperly placed, the reflection is not seen.

The example of Rahu (Node), a real thing, is quoted to prove that a real thing may be seen at certain times and may not be seen at certain other times. In that case we learn about the reality of Rahu from Scriptures before we actually see it. Secondly, according to those who hold that Rahu is but the shadow of the Earth, it cannot be a real thing, as the unreality of the shadow has already been established.

THE EXPERIENCER OF TRANSMIGRATORY EXISTENCE

Transmigratory existence cannot be predicated of the Pure Self by virtue of Its being actionless; nor can it be predicated of the ego which is, devoid of a real existence, not a conscious entity. The only plausible explanation is that transmigratory existence is due to lack of proper discrimination between the Pure Self and the non-Self. Nevertheless, transmigratory existence has always an apparent existence solely due to the real existence of the Self, and further, appears to belong to the Self owing to indiscrimination. That is like the apparent existence had by the rope-snake on the basis of the reality of the rope, of course, prior to the discrimination between the rope and the snake.

It is only the people who cannot discriminate between the real and the unreal, between the Pure Self, Its reflection and the Intellect, who hold that the eternal Self is changeful on account of the modifications in the mind pertaining to It and is the experiencer of the transmigratory existence. They have no real understanding of the scriptures. They hold or mistake the ego to be the Self.

WORDS IMPLYING THE SELF

The Vedas do imply the Self by the use of words like Knowledge, Existence, etc. There the implication becomes reasonable because the Self is of the nature of Pure Consciousness and Intellect has got the reflection of the Self in it. These words are directly applied to the Intellect carrying the reflection of the Pure Self in it and indirectly to the Pure Self.

It can be said that in words like 'Karoti' (He does), 'Gacchati' (He goes) etc., the Prakriti Artha of the Dhatu (meaning of the verb, it denotes an action) and the Pratyaya Artha (meaning of the verbal suffix, it denotes agency) belong to one and the same subject according to grammarians and laymen, whereas in words like 'Jaanaati' (He knows), the verb meaning and the meaning of the suffix denote two different subjects. The latter, exceptional case as it is, needs explanation.

In words like 'Jaanaati,' the meaning of the verbal suffix that involves an agent has reference to the reflection of the

Self in the intellect and the meaning of the verb that involves an action has reference to a particular modification of the intellect. Due to indiscrimination between the reflection of the Self and the intellect, the word 'Knows' is wrongly applied to the Self. In reality, the intellect by itself, is devoid of consciousness and the Self is devoid of action; the word 'Knows' cannot be predicated of either of them on any reasonable ground whatsoever.

Knowledge construed to mean the action of knowing cannot be attributed to the eternal Self that is actionless. Knowledge in the sense of an instrument of the action of knowing can be applied only to the intellect and not to the Self. Possession of instrument implies agency and agency cannot be attributed to Self that is actionless. Neither can the word be applied to the Self in the senses of that which is the object of the action of knowing.

The Self is never knowable as an object, and is not denoted by any word directly by those who hold It to be Changeless, Actionless, Eternal and One only.

If the ego were the Self, then a word can be applied to it in its (the word's) primary meaning, Vachyartha. But, that position can never be had on account of scriptural passages that state that the Self is free from hunger, thirst, etc. That reduces us to the position that the primary meaning of words are not applicable. That means that words having no primary meaning cannot have secondary (Lakshya) ones, too. In that case, the Vedas, too, will lose their authority, inasmuch as they will be using meaningless words; and that position is not desirable. Solving this problem will land us in a dilemma.

To accept the popular usage of words is to accept the doctrine of the Charvakas and take the body to be the Self. To accept the view of the learned is to arrive at the dilemma that a word cannot be applied to the intellect which is devoid of consciousness, and likewise, to the Self which is devoid of action. Neither can it be said that the authoritative Vedas use meaningless words.

People use words like 'Knows' etc. without proper discrimination between the reflecting medium (intellect) and that which is reflected (the Self). Agency is attributed to the Self in using words like 'Knows' etc. on account of the superimposition of the agency of the intellect upon the Self. Likewise, the intellect is called the Knower owing to the Superimposition of the Conscious Self upon it (the intellect). In short, there exists Paraspara-Adhyasa. Consciousness belongs to the Pure Self, of which action cannot be predicated. Knowledge is eternal and is identical with the Self; the intellect cannot create it. Persons who hold that knowledge is produced (and thereby predicate agency in the act of knowing etc. of the intellect) are merely deluded by the modifications of a non-conscious intellect that appears to be conscious.

To sum up, though, strictly speaking, words like 'Knows' etc. cannot be applied either to the intellect or the Self, their application is rendered possible owing to indiscrimination between the Self, the intellect and the reflection of the Self in the intellect.

NEED TO ASSUME A REFLECTION OF THE SELF

Certain schools of Buddhism hold that there exists no witness other than the modifications of the intellect, which modifications are, by themselves, both the perceivers and the perceived. Even if we are to accept the need for a Knower to these modifications who will be constant (Knower should be the same in respect to all modifications, as based on the evidence of recognition, on the evidence of the inherent capacity to synthesise all modifications and relate it to one individual) and who will know or witness the presence or otherwise of these modifications, some schools of Vedantins hold that there is no need to assume a reflection of the Self.

Accepting this knower cannot solve the problem, for, when once agency is predicated of it in the act of knowing, it comes under the non-conscious group. Similarly, dispensing with the reflection of the Self, it cannot be argued that these modifications are known by themselves due to their proximity to the eternal Knower, the Self. The Changeless, Actionless Knower—Self is of no utility. If proximity to the eternal Self be the sole factor in mental modifications being known by themselves, then, we should grant mental modifications to all insentient beings since the eternal Knower-Self is all-pervading.

TO WHOM IS THE TEACHING THOU ART THAT?

Who is the aspirant to whom the words 'Thou Art That' are addressed? Who suffers pain and misery in ignorance and stands in need of the teaching 'Thou Art That?' The aspirant cannot be the eternal Witness Itself since It is untouched by ignorance and its effects. The aspirant cannot be either an agent. In that case, he cannot accept the idea, 'I am Brahman, the Witness.' As a result, the teaching 'Thou Art That' becomes a falsity and that position is not acceptable. The teaching can nevertheless be accepted, provided we grant indiscrimination due to ignorance between ego and the Self to the Sruti when it declares 'Tat Tvam Asi.'

Should the Sruti discriminate between the ego and the Self, the foregoing defect arises, namely, that an agent to an action cannot be admitted to be the Witness. If it be said, like the Samkhyas, that the word 'Thou' finally refers to the Witness, the relation between the ego and the Self, in the absence of a reflection of the Self, should be established so that the word 'Thou' can have the implied

RIGHT SIGNIFICANCE OF 'TAT TVAM ASI'

meaning referring to the Witness.

The relation cannot be one of the Seer and the Seen, for it cannot be admitted in the case of the Witness which is devoid of activity. Neither can it be said that there exists an identity between the ego and the Witness though the latter is devoid of activity; there being no opportunity for the knowledge pertaining to that identity to exist in the absence of the knowledge of the relation that my Self, the Witness exists. The relationship cannot also be known through the scriptures on the following three grounds, viz., (a) The ego cannot know the relation as it is unconscious, (b) similarly in the case of the Witness-Self because It is changeless and actionless, and (c) the non-conscious ego cannot be taught by the Sruti. Granting that there still exists a relation between the ego and the Self, the knowledge of such relation can only be one of 'mine' and in no case one of identity.

To accept that the non-conscious intellect appears to be conscious, is to accept that the modifications of the intellect also appear to be so like sparks of red-hot iron. It should be noted that the act of pervading the intellect on the part of the Self-Witness, like fire pervading a mass of iron, is not a *change* on the part of the Self; the same has been refuted in the example of the mirror and the face. Further, it should be understood that an illustration and its subject can nowhere bear absolute similarity in all respects.

CONCLUSION

The knowledge on the part of the people of the appearance of the mental modifications and the disappearance of the same is possible on reasonable grounds only on account of (a) the existence of the Witness-Consciousness-Self and (b) the Limit (after a certain limit, the Self alone exists when everything else is negated). And on the acceptance of the reflection of the Self, it can be admitted that the intellect may know itself to be Brahman, for words that denote directly the reflection of the Self or the ego and other things which reflect the Self, indirectly imply the eternal Self. It has already been stated that the reflection is not real.

Nowhere in the Scriptures has it been stated that intellect is conscious; in that case, if it be conscious, we should attribute consciousness to the physical body and the senses too. Then the position of Charvakas comes in and that is neither desirable nor acceptable.

If the intellect be insentient, as it is, then in the absence of a reflection, the knowledge 'I am Brahman' is not possible. The teaching 'Tat Tvam Asi' will become useless as a result, i.e., in the absence of the possibility for the existence of the knowledge 'I Am Brahman.'

Therefore, the teaching 'Tat Tvam Asi' is only for those who can discriminate between the Self and the non-Self and who can understand the word 'thou' to directly mean the reflection of the Self in the intellect and indirectly to imply the eternal Self.